The Secret Chord

Peter Banks & Jonathan Evens

Copyright © 2012 Peter Banks and Jonathan Evens

Peter Banks and Jonathan Evens have asserted their moral rights to be identified as the author of this work under the Copyright, Designs and Patents Act 1988.

All rights reserved. Which means thou shalt not steal any of our hard graft to reproduce, store or transmit any of this work's content in any way, shape or form without asking nicely. Up to 400 words may be used for the purposes of critical review or recommendation.

This work may be read out aloud to individuals or groups as long as the performance is not recorded onto any storage medium.

The front cover was created by Peter Banks using a Phoster App template and features a modified version of the chord created by Mikhail Abraham, aka Hyacinth, from Professor Jason Brown's analysis.

THE HOLY BIBLE, NEW INTERNATIONAL VERSION®, NIV® Copyright © 1973, 1978, 1984, 2011 by Biblica, Inc.™ Used by permission. All rights reserved worldwide.

All hyperlinks and more information on:

www.thesecretchord.co.uk

ISBN 978-1-291-08379-8

Inspiration and Perspiration

"Don't only practice your art, but force your way into its secrets, for it and knowledge can raise men to the divine."

Ludwig van Beethoven

"I really enjoyed the book. It's well written, full of wisdom, great quotes and illustrations. It's great to read something about art and Christianity that embraces such diverse material."

**Revd Dr Hugh Rayment-Pickard
author and co-founder of IntoUniversity**

"This is an interesting and impassioned study of the role of music in cultural life, written through the prism of a Christian belief which conveys a great enthusiasm for music and its transformative powers."

Carol Biss Managing Director of Book Guild Publishing

To be inspired is something to seek after, to earnestly desire. It sometimes comes to those who seek, more often it happens when witnessing an extraordinary gift that seems to have been given only to some. These are the inspirational ones. Remember, with affection, those that have gone before and endeavour to rejoice with these, our contemporaries.

Peter Banks - 2012

The Authors

Peter Banks is a successful composer and musician with mainstream chart successes in many countries in the world within his most well known musical collaboration, After The Fire. As well as a musician he has worked in other creative industries and now contributes professionally to various online publications as well as his popular music and technology blog, The BanksyBoy Brief.

Jonathan Evens is a Vicar in East London who integrates his creative writing and painting into his ministry. A keen blogger he posts regularly on issues of faith and culture. His journalism and art criticism ranges from A.W.N. Pugin to U2 and has been published by publications including Art & Christianity and Church Times. He runs a visual arts organisation called commission4mission (c4m) which encourages churches to commission contemporary art and, together with fellow c4m artist Henry Shelton, has published Mark of the Cross, a collection of meditations and images on Christ's Passion.

CONTENTS

Inspiration and Perspiration	3
The Authors	5
Introduction	8
Sacred versus Secular?	11
Muse versus Market	23
Play versus Plan	35
Medium versus Message	50
Chaos versus Connection	64
Head versus Heart	86
Search versus Stasis	99
In Conclusion	111
Notes and Bibliography	117

[I]
Introduction

Leonard Cohen's song 'Hallelujah' makes the claim that the Biblical King David had found a secret chord which, when played, pleased even God himself. Given the longevity which Cohen's song has achieved through the numerous recordings by diverse artists of "cover"[1] versions – from X Factor winners to the soundtrack of Shrek – it might be thought that Cohen has found the secret of transcending demographics. But that is not what the song or Cohen claim. Is there really a "Secret Chord" that would both please the Lord and nearly everybody else? And are there some people who just don't get or care for music, as the next line of Cohen's lyric also suggests?

Sometimes music really divides opinion, at other times it appears to break down tribal boundaries and cultivate harmony in the same way sport can. But what is it that causes these phenomena? Is it actually the music, the context to which it is associated, is it simply a matter of taste, preference for a particular style or something else altogether? Are there common denominators in some music that transcend cultural and geographic boundaries? What extent does the time, place (i.e. venue), environment, timing and audience make to the impact of a particular piece when it is rendered? And this is in addition to the variable musical parameters such as tempo, performers and arrangement.

The opening words to Cohen's song are extrapolated from an early Biblical account[2] of how King Saul (1079 BC – 1007 BC) asked for a skilful musician to be found so they could come and play to soothe Saul's troubled soul. It is clear that David was both a competent musician and also a prolific composer. According to the Scriptures, he would go on to curate and compose many of the 150 Psalms found in the Bible which survive in multiple translations as part of religious worship today. What Cohen is surmising is that whatever David played, or, most likely, improvised, would have also pleased the LORD[3], the children of Israel's God, as well as calming down King Saul. Additionally Cohen's romantic hypothesis is that David had actually stumbled across and therefore deliberately employed a particular chord (a collection of notes played together) that has this mysterious power.

This begs another question, that, if there is, indeed, a Secret Chord, a bit like the Golden Section[4] in Greek architecture, then surely most composers would both be aware of it and incorporate it in their work to achieve instant appreciation?

However, research has shown there is not much known about the possible music David played despite the many melodies passed down by an oral tradition within Jewish communities and the explicit instructions the composer gives to "The Director of Music" for many of the Psalms. Furthermore the combination of musical tuning and notes (also known as intervals) may well have been different from what is accepted as a standard in the western world.

So even though there are many pieces of music that use similar structures and sequences of chords and melodies that may possibly provide some way toward a quest to find the Secret Chord, we cannot assume what David played for King Saul back then would be as instantly soothing to our ear nowadays.

Furthermore Cohen, in the next lyrical line, may be tipping his hat towards a generation gap in musical taste where the phrase "I don't know how you can listen to that noise" demonstrates a gulf emerging in artistic appreciation!

Exploring questions such as these are what this book is about. In it we are seeking to explore a number of the dilemmas which musicians and other artists face, not so much in order to map out one route through or around these dilemmas but in an attempt to get the creative juices flowing. Our experience of creativity is of disparate and often contradictory ideas being crushed, swirled, fermented, shaken AND stirred in our minds in order that the fine wine of creativity results. Those disparate and often contradictory ideas are a little like the grit in the oyster which eventually produces the pearl or possibly, in this instance, the Secret Chord. Our hope is that this book, by exploring artistic dilemmas from a range of different perspectives, will mature in people's minds exactly like that delicious wine or precious pearl.

[1]
Sacred versus Secular?

In the early days of rock 'n' roll a unique event occurred; four of the biggest stars, at the time, happened to all be in the same recording studio Tuesday December 4, 1956 . They were Carl Perkins, Jerry Lee-Lewis, Johnny Cash and Elvis Presley. They were not there to record but they did start a "jam session"[5]. Someone left the tapes rolling, recorded their jamming and later released it under the title of *The Million Dollar Quartet* [6].

So what did these four rock 'n' rollers sing when they got together for this impromptu jam session? They sang hymns and country gospel songs. Because they all grew up in Southern Pentecostal Churches they drew on a shared background of Spirituals, Gospel and the charismata of Southern Pentecostalism[7]. As a result of this shared background, each faced anxiety over their decisions to substitute what they deemed as "secular" words and movements for sacred songs and mannerisms.

This was particularly apparent in the life of Jerry Lee-Lewis. After Jerry started playing piano, his mother enrolled him in the Southwestern Assemblies of God University so that her son would exclusively sing songs to the Lord. But at a University talent show Jerry played some "worldly" music and next day was expelled by the Dean. Years later one of his fellow students asked Jerry "Are you still playing the devil's music?" Jerry replied "Yes, I am. But you know it's strange, the same music that they kicked me out of school for is the same kind of music they play in their churches today. The difference is, I know I am playing for the devil and they don't". [8] The beginnings of rock 'n' roll were felt as a betrayal of sacred music by those involved and by the Churches that judged them.

Something similar occurred as Soul music developed out of Black Gospel. Ray Charles began a trend which was later successfully followed by the like of Sam Cooke and Aretha Franklin, among many others, when he introduced gospel-singing techniques into his vocal style and adapted church-based songs into R&B hits. Tony Cummings writes:

> From James Brown to Diana Ross, black singers consistently show their origins to be a storefront church in Harlem or Macon or Detroit ... it's a cliché. Every soul artist interviewed seems to have an identikit story – "I was always interested in music. I sang in a church choir".[9]

Laura Barton has written about the way in which the music, the themes and language but also the delivery, the oratory, the rhythm and drama of the Sunday sermon informed the mainstream music of Jackie Wilson, Sam Cooke, Percy Sledge, Al Green, James Brown, Little Richard, among others:

> The sermon style of the African-American church has always been markedly different from that of the white

church – the theologian Dr Hughes Oliphant Old has noted how the white church "produces literature rather than oratory. Its sermons appeal to the eye, that is, the eye of the one reading the sermon, rather than to the ear of the one hearing it". In the black church, however, the appeal is primarily to the ear – the preacher taking a formulaic sermon and using a variety of oratorical techniques to conjure a kind of devotional intensity: improvisation, repetition, reinforcement, dramatic pauses, hemistich cadence, parallelism, the act of call-and-response harnessing that relationship between the preacher and the congregation, the individual and the community. It brings a rhythm that is not so much a meter as a pulse, a sermon that seems not just words on a page but a living, breathing creation.[10]

The movement hasn't been exclusively one way, however. The soul star Al Green is one of those who has felt the tension between flesh and Spirit, secular and sacred. He left a multi-million dollar career to sing Gospel and, in the film *The Gospel According To Al Green*, explains that he was "moved by the Spirit" that led him to leave his so-called "secular", mainstream recording career to sing Gospel and to pastor a Church. His decision freed him to sing exclusively about the light that he had found in Jesus Christ and to preach the Gospel as he did so. Because of his past career and because he continued to sing his old hits he was able to continue to sing to people outside the church as well as to the faithful inside but for many who, like Al Green, want to sing exclusively about the light that they have found in Jesus that opportunity is not extended. They decide to make their living in what became labelled as "Contemporary Christian Music" (hereafter CCM).

CCM is a fascinating sociological phenomenon as it is a separate category of music with its own record labels sold in alternative retail outlets, mainly known as "Christian Bookshops", and appeals primarily to Church-based audiences whilst encompassing many genres and styles of music. The irony of CCM is that is if you want to sing exclusively about the "Light" and to evangelise from that stage you end up singing principally to the already-converted.

The artiste Larry Norman was often thought of as one of the founding figures of CCM yet actually began his career recording for mainstream record labels and singing songs that both named the name of Jesus and critiqued the society in which he lived. As a pioneer in writing Rock music explicitly from the perspective of a Christian, he attracted criticism from the Church and from the record industry with critics claiming that he was "too rock and roll for the Church and too religious for the rock and rollers". Eventually, the pressure from the record companies became too much and he launched his own record label which played an important role in establishing the separate strand of music with the CCM tag.

It doesn't have to be like this, however. Johnny Cash was one of the Million Dollar Quartet who went on to have an eventful life which included divorce, drug abuse, imprisonment and conversion to Christianity (among many other things!). For Cash, returning to his Christian faith was one of the factors that eventually made possible the overcoming of his addictions giving him the ability to continue a career which culminated in the critically acclaimed series of albums called *American Recordings* that he made towards the end of his life.

On these albums he sang songs from every stage of his life, singing about love, murder and God. He covered songs, like "Hurt", written by Trent Reznor of Nine Inch Nails, which were thought of as "secular" yet, through his interpretation, drew out their inherent spirituality. By doing so, he could be seen as redeeming his culture – popular culture – and reversing the adoption of sacred songs for secular causes which had been a significant part of the birth of rock 'n' roll. He sang honestly and affectingly of sin and the salvation that comes through repentance[11].

While he sang openly about his faith and the strength it gave him, no one listening felt like they were being preached at. People identified with the way the songs were stripped down musically and emotionally, with the honest and open way in which Cash sang of what his life had been like and the wisdom he had gained from living it.

It was possible for him to do this because the music of the South – American Music - has always been shot through with the awareness of sin and salvation. "Rock & roll was born in the American South," wrote Bill Flanagan in his book *Written On My Soul*, "The whole history of rock & roll could be told in Southern accents, from the delta bluesmen and country troubadours to the Baptist gospel singers and Okie folkies".[12]

The South, as the novelist Flannery O'Connor wrote, "is Christ-haunted". To see the extent to which this is true watch the film *Searching for the Wrong-Eyed Jesus* in which alternative country singer-songwriter Jim White takes a tour of the South as he knows it. He shows us desperate people with a hell-fire religion and a God who will "whup the ass" of those who prefer the sinful flesh over the Holy Spirit. But here, he claims, you also feel the presence of the Spirit – it's alive and awake and in the blood of those who live in the South.

"Do you like American music?" the Violent Femmes asked on their fifth album *Why Do Birds Sing?* They answered in the affirmative but the reason they gave seems a pretty weird one; that every time they look in the ugly lake of American music it reminds them of themselves.

The idea of American music as a lake reflecting an ugly self isn't the only strange definition that's been given though. This is the picture of traditional American music conjured up by Bob Dylan in 1966: "Traditional music is based on hexagrams. It comes from legends, bibles, plagues, and it revolves around vegetables and death. ... All these songs about roses growing out of people's brains and lovers who are really geese and swans that turn into angels - they're not going to die. .... I mean, you'd think that the traditional music people could gather from their songs that mystery is a fact, a traditional fact ... In that music is the only true, valid death you can feel today off a record player. .... It has to do with a purity thing. I think its meaninglessness is holy".[13]

Greil Marcus has pointed out that this "traditional music", the ancient ballads of mountain music, songs like Buell Kazee's East Virginia, Clarence Ashley's Coo Coo Bird or Dock Boggs' Country Blues - are what Dylan and the Band tapped into when recording *The Basement Tapes*, *John Wesley Harding* and *The Band*, music which Marcus describes as a "kaleidoscope of American music". The "acceptance of death" that Dylan found in "traditional music," says Marcus, "is simply a singer's insistence on mystery as inseparable from any honest understanding of what life is all about; it is the quiet terror of a man seeking salvation who stares into a void that stares back".[14] Or a lake that reflects an ugly self?

But maybe that's only one half of the picture. Anything that comes from bibles and where swans turn into angels can't be all void and ugliness, can't be all bad. In 1985 Dylan expanded on the fundamental impact of the Bible on America and on his work: "... the Bible runs through all U.S. life, whether people know it or not. It's the founding book. The founding fathers' book anyway. People can't get away from it. You can't get away from it wherever you go. Those ideas were true then and they're true now. They're scriptural, spiritual laws. I guess people can read into that what they want. But if they're familiar with those concepts they'll probably find enough of them in my stuff. Because I

17

always get back to that".[15] Maybe what you get in traditional American music is that combination of sin and salvation that Californian troubadour Peter Case said characterised his debut album.

Dylan maintained back in 1966 that this kind of American music was not going to die so where can we find it in reasonably contemporary company? There are a loosely affiliated group of bands and songwriters - T. Bone Burnett, Peter Case, Mark Heard, The Innocence Mission, Maria McKee, Julie & Buddy Miller, Sam Phillips, Sixteen Horsepower, Violent Femmes, Gillian Welch, Jim White, Victoria Williams - for whom fear and threat, mystery and enamour - the twin poles of American music – show up again and again in their music and in relationships. The affiliations between these artists branch out in a way that cries out for a Rock Family Tree mapping production, songwriting and session credits together with personal relationships.

In this way, too, they take us back to Dylan, The Band, *The Basement Tapes* and Greil Marcus' surely incomplete statement that they show "the quiet terror of a man seeking salvation who stares into a void that stares back". The whole point about *The Basement Tapes* was that a bunch of mates sat around making the music they loved the way they loved it and when they liked. If Dylan was staring into a void then he wasn't doing it alone. And wasn't this true too of the music that they drew on, that it was more the music of a community than of individuals? We talk more about Appalachian traditions or the bluegrass Bristol area of

Tennessee and East Carolina than we do about Dock Boggs or Clarence Ashley. A relational approach to work and life seems important to Williams, Burnett, Heard and the other musicians that share their musical vision and this is so although their relationships feature brokenness, pain and loss. Relationships and a community of music makers seem a vital part then of this tradition of American music.

So there we have it. Fear and threat on the one hand, mystery and enamour on the other - the twin poles of American music. Legends, bibles, plagues, vegetables and death, roses growing out of people's brains, lovers who are really geese and swans that turn into angels - they're all in the mix. These are songs of sin and salvation as sung by the wild, unshod, soot-covered orphans of God.

This interplay between the "sacred" and the "secular" in rock music is not exclusive to it. Instead it is indicative of an interplay also found in classical and choral music traditions. Church composers, as incumbents under patronage, would regularly insert tunes taken from bawdy folk songs into their weekly Mass settings knowing that these tunes would both be recognised and their incongruity appreciated by the congregation. Meanwhile the clergy would remain blissfully oblivious to anything drawn from popular, contemporary culture and the irony thereof!

In contrast William Booth, the founder of the Salvation Army, famously proclaimed, "Why should the Devil have all the best tunes". For his Christmas message to *War Cry* readers of 1880 Booth wrote:

> Secular music, do you say, belongs to the devil? Does it? Well, if it did I would plunder him for it, for he has no right to a single note of the whole seven... Every note, and every strain, and every harmony is divine, and belongs to us... So consecrate your voice and your instruments. Bring out your cornets and harps and organs and flutes and violins and pianos and drums, and everything else that can make melody. Offer them to God, and use them to make all the hearts about you merry before the Lord.[16]

It is intriguing that Booth mentions only seven notes which we can assume are C D E F G A B of the major key. This implies he may have been suggesting that minor keys and accidentals should be avoided, both very much being a feature of the blues and jazz music genres.

Additionally Booth's approach is one which has always attracted criticism within the Church, in terms characterised by the following quote:

> I'm no music scholar, but I feel I know appropriate church music when I hear it. Last Sunday's new song, if you can call it that, sounded like a sentimental love ballad, one you'd expect to hear crooned in a bar. If you insist on exposing us to rubbish like this, in Gods house, don't be surprised if many of the faithful look for a new place to worship. The hymns we grew up with are all we need.[17]

That was written in 1863 about the hymn *Just As I Am* but could just as easily have been a critique of contemporary compositions to accompany current church worship. Such critics fail to understand or even to acknowledge the interplay in music between what is generally understood as "secular" and what is generally understood as "sacred".

Leonard Cohen's *Hallelujah* includes both the sacred and the sinful – the holy and the broken Hallelujah. It doesn't matter which you heard, he suggests, because a blaze of light is found in every word and he will be able to stand before God – the Lord of Song – presumably at the Last Judgement and simply sing Hallelujah itself because both the holy and the broken are encapsulated in the one word and one chord.

Whilst Cohen works with this popular distinction of "sacred" and "secular" by writing about both the holy and broken Hallelujah he suggests that, in conclusion, it doesn't actually matter which we hear, as both are Hallelujahs. Ultimately, he will stand before the Lord of Song and there will no distinctions, just a Hallelujah on his tongue. Presumably, it could be either the holy or the broken Hallelujah? It simply doesn't matter to us or to the Lord of Song.

This is to say, then, that distinctions between sacred and secular are false divides creating on the one hand Christian ghettos which are always one or more steps behind popular culture, as demonstrated in services using a more contemporary style of worship music which currently (in 2011/12) sound like Coldplay or Keane "Lite", or, on the other hand, which induce the kind of guilt that we have seen in Jerry Lee Lewis and Al Green by singing what is perceived to be the devil's music. In that respect Peter maintains:

> "There's not necessarily a right (sacred) or wrong (secular) way, oftentimes there is a better way".

That better way is described well by David Adam:

> We need to reveal that our God is in all the world and waits to be discovered there – or, to be more exact, the world is in Him, all is in the heart of God. Our work, our travels, our joys and our sorrows are enfolded in His loving care. We cannot for a moment fall out of the hands of God. Typing pool and workshop, office and factory are all as sacred as the church. The presence of God pervades the work place as much as He does a church sanctuary.[18]

The presence of God pervades music as much as the work place or a church sanctuary. Elvis is quoted as saying, "God loves you, but He loves you best when you sing".[19] Note, not just when you sing "sacred" songs; although whether Elvis realised that himself is open to question!

[2]
Muse versus Market

Impresario Simon Cowell has argued that no one has the right to say that they have better taste than those who watch his shows "because essentially what you're doing is calling millions of people morons". What this ignores, however, is that his shows are expressly designed and planned to attract and retain the largest possible audience to such an extent that the audience willingly pays the producers, through the voting system, to provide market research information which is then used to guide and shape the subsequent career of the eventual victor. The immediate outcome of this marketing research information is a lucrative and almost guaranteed Christmas No. 1.

X Factor, for example, road tests singers and song styles with a national audience over several months encouraging the audience not simply to enjoy performances but to identify with the journey taken by their chosen star over the course of the show. Every aspect of this process is designed to build a market for the eventual winner and make money for those who own the rights to the show and performers. Everything in X Factor is market driven and designed thereby, as Sting argued in a 2009 interview for the Evening Standard, making genuine spontaneity, individuality, eccentricity and originality absent by default:

> I tried to keep an open mind, but basically I was looking at televised karaoke where they conform to stereotypes. They are either Mariah Carey or Whitney Houston or Boyzone and are not encouraged to create any real unique signature or fingerprint.[20]

This is music at its most mercantile. Contrast that with a vision of music as the symbol of ultimate creativity. In the depiction of creation found in *The Magician's Nephew*, C. S. Lewis shows us his God character, Aslan, creating the land of Narnia through song:

> The Lion was pacing to and fro about that empty land and singing his new song. It was softer and more lilting than the song by which he had called up the stars and the sun; a gentle, rippling music. And as he walked and sang the valley grew green with grass. It spread out from the Lion like a pool. It ran up the sides of the little hills like a wave. In a few minutes it was creeping up the lower slopes of the distant mountains, making that young world every moment softer ... all this time the Lion's song, and his stately prowl, to and fro, backwards and forwards, was going on ... Polly was finding the song more and more interesting because she thought she was beginning to see the connection between the music and the things that were happening. When a line of dark firs sprang up on a ridge about a hundred yards away she felt

that they were connected with a series of deep, prolonged notes which the Lion had sung a second before. And when he burst into a rapid series of lighter notes she was not surprised to see primroses suddenly appearing in every direction. Thus, with an unspeakable thrill, she felt quite certain that all the things were coming (as she said) "out of the Lion's head". When you listened to his song you heard the things he was making up: when you looked round you, you saw them. This was so exciting that she had no time to be afraid.

This is an image also found in Bruce Cockburn's "Creation Dream" where, in vision, he sees the creative Christ singing creation into being by means of lines of power which burst outward along the channels of the song he sings.

If music is a symbol of the means by which God created the universe, then the musician is a partner with God in the creative process; a prayer that we also find Cockburn articulating as he asks the creative Christ - that glittering joker who dances in the jaws of the dragon – if he can be just a little of his creative breath as it moves over the waters of chaos - the face of the deep – to bring all things into being.

Cockburn suggests that those who love have the ability to hear music that is beyond the normal range of human hearing - too high for the human ear – and to see in ways which pierce the apparent darkness of night to encounter a purity beyond our imaging. In other words to see and hear life as God sees and hears it and to articulate something of that vision. Similarly, in her novel *Children of God*, Mary Doria Russell writes of Isaac discovering the music of DNA, which is God's music. Andrey Tarkovsky wrote that "The poet does not use 'descriptions' of the world; he himself has a hand in its creation".[21] He also quotes Dostoevesky as saying, "the writer (poet) himself creates life such as it has never quite been before him".[22]

Dorothy L. Sayers developed similar ideas further in "The Mind of the Maker" suggesting that the creative process itself (idea, implementation and interaction) reveals the Trinitarian nature of the creative force behind all things. Timothy Hyman makes a similar proposal when he suggests that:

> One of the best ways to think of a great work of art is to see it as a fusion, parallel to the Trinity, of intellect, matter and spirit – of the abstract, the physical and the emotional – of reason and humanity and energy – all held in perfect balance.

With such a sublime vision of the Arts one might expect church services (of divine worship) to share such sublimity, yet it is arguable that much of the aforementioned contemporary worship shares more with the mercantile vision of X Factor than it does with Cockburn's prayer. That, at least, is the contention of one musician:

> Worship songs are "shipped in" to many churches. Every now and again they get a new delivery all the way from California or Australia (and Sussex!). Like

crates of Coca Cola being delivered. Now Cola is nice to drink once in a while, theoretically I've got nothing against it, but what about local ale or beautifully matured wine from the local vineyard; real food that we all cook together here and now? Where are the songs of *that* church? *That* town? *Their* hearts? How good would it be for people to find *their* song, not the X Factor, big screen, 'every song sounds the same' song.[23]

The author Nick Page has made similar critiques of contemporary worship songs in his excellent book, *And now let's move into a time of nonsense*[24]. He argues that worship songs don't last because no one expects them to:

> They're not created with any expectation or hope of longevity; they're written on the understanding that they will suffer a quick death. They're the spiritual equivalent of the paper plate. They serve their purpose, but it's time to throw away the old and move on. This is a consumerist, superficial idea of worship; the idea that once a song has been used up we can throw it away. The idea of dwelling on a lyric, of contemplating it, is almost unimaginable. What is there to contemplate? It's a disposable product.

This view of worship is unconsciously supported by those who make, market and distribute worship songs as a commercial activity because they are always needing to 'ship' in the latest delivery of new songs in order to remain commercially viable. Nick Page concludes:

> We have a church that is addicted to newness, part of a culture which worships continuous consumption, and in the pop song we have found the perfect model for the easy-come, easy-go worship song. What's top of the charts this week will be forgotten next week; don't worry if you've forgotten the words of the song you've just sung, there'll be another one along in a minute. It's fast-food worship; fine at the time, but half an hour later you feel hungry all over again.

A deeply profound song from Jackson Browne is one of Peter's favourite Christmas pieces with so much truth and depth compared to other commercial offerings that are often sung in churches. Browne links "Temple Trading"[25] to both the Church and environmental issues way back in the early nineties when the song was written. Browne writes a litany of phrases used by Christians in worship – "Prince of Peace", "The Saviour" – as he pictures the pride, boldness and faith with which Christians have prayed to him while sailing the world's seas to fill Churches with gold taken from other lands. Such actions, he states, can be condemned from the very mouth of Jesus – the rebel Jesus – who said that the world in which he worshipped had been turned from a temple to a robber's den by such trading.

In the last verse he apologises for appearing to be judgemental (which may be another aposite sideswipe at the established church!) before closing the song with the fantastic proclamation that he bids us Christmas cheer and pleasure as a heathen and pagan who is, nevertheless, on the side of the rebel Jesus. This is because Jesus also opposes the exploitation of others, especially when passed off as being done in the name of worship.

Given that "art expresses the ideal and man's aspiration towards the infinite", the late Russian film maker Tarkovsky writes, "it cannot be harnessed to consumerist aims without being violated in its very nature". Accordingly, he also wrote that it seemed to him "meaningless and futile to reckon the 'success' of a film arithmetically, in terms of seats sold". One could say the same, perhaps, of numbers at church services!

Tarkovsky's final film *The Sacrifice* was conceived as a response to materialism:

> What moved me was the theme of harmony that is born of sacrifice, the twofold dependence of love ... I am interested above all in the character who is capable of sacrificing himself and his way of life ... Such behaviour precludes, by its very nature, all of those selfish interests that make up a 'normal' rationale for action; it refutes the laws of a materialistic worldview ... the more clearly I discerned the stamp of materialism on the face of our planet (irrespective of whether I was observing the West or the East), came up against unhappy people, saw the victims of

psychoses symptomatic of an inability or unwillingness to see why life had lost all delight and all value, why it had become oppressive, the more committed I felt to this film as the most important thing in my life.[26]

And yet commercial viability cannot be ignored in supporting creative expression. The art organisation with which Jonathan is involved, commission4mission,[27] has been set up to enable local churches to commission contemporary art despite the financial constraints they face. While Peter's band, After The Fire,[28] originally split up after their record company withdrew their tour support putting the band a further £36k in debt (in total ~£300k, a small fortune back in 1982!) when they were determined to go on and finish their tour. This was despite mainstream achievements that were unprecedented in the UK at that time for a band whose members were known to be Christians and whose faith was subtly expressed in and through their music. Ironically, commercial success unexpectedly followed the decision to split appearing just at the point when the band members themselves were unable to capitalise.

Such ironies had begun earlier in their career as they pioneered writing love songs able to be understood both as declarations of love in boy/girl relationships and also as cries of devotion towards God. However, after the release of Bob Dylan's *Slow Train Coming*, they were called into the office by management and warned they must become more direct with their lyrics as "it's (songs with explicitly Christian lyrics) selling".

Grayson Perry has spoken helpfully about the inhibiting nature of commercial success on professional visual artists:

> Serious play is what I do and as a child it pours out of you. And then you become self-conscious and then, if you become a professional artist, you're even more self-conscious because not only have you got the, 'Am I doing the right thing?' Am I doing the right thing in public? With all of the weight of contemporary and art history down on you ... If you want to become a successful artist you've got to learn to still be able to play when you've got a camera over your shoulder and a gallery dealer and a public and a collector all looking at what you're doing and saying is it going to be, you know, and you're still trying to play like a kid in the bedroom with nobody even knowing you're doing it.[29]

Bruce Springsteen, on his *We Shall Overcome - The Seeger Sessions / American Land Edition* identifies a difference between performers who simply 'play' music and those that 'make' music together which may help to translate Perry's observation from the world of visual art to that of music. As the interview progresses it is clear that Springsteen is referring to the way some players are not content to just interpret a music score (or chord / tab chart) – as do, for example, those who perform on *The X Factor* - but have the inherent gift to gel together with their fellow musicians such that a new plane is reached where communication is instinctive rather than reactive. The group of players effectively become one and feel the groove enabling co-ordinated variations and improvisations with no pre-meditation.

Such moments transcend commercial considerations and historically it is clear when such moments occur – either as musical conventions are challenged or there is an 'ethnic' re-imagination - then substantial musical developments occur. In relatively recent times we have seen the advent of Jazz, the worldwide success of songwriting bands spearheaded by The Beatles and then the Punk explosion. Equally there has been the international popularity of Reggae and Gospel Music on one hand and the UK folk music's crossover into the mainstream with groups such as The Fishermen Friends with their repertoire of traditional shanties. There is a potential division between classical and popular music performers that disappears when both have the grace and desire to side-step such differences. Such developments occur when musicians actively listen to one another and by doing so achieve a performance and response that transcends any which would have been achieved had the artistes chosen to stay either entrenched or simply played safe/commercial.

Nick Coleman, the former NME journalist, describes, in his entertaining yet deeply moving memoir *The Train in the Night: A Story of Music and Loss*,[30] how his world was changed forever when he was diagnosed as having the condition Sudden Neurosensory Hearing Loss, a combination of partial deafness combined with thunderous tinnitus. He effectively had to re-learn how to hear and for some time during his recovery it was his encyclopaedic knowledge of pop, rock and classical music that sustained him as he psychologically engineered a way to replay his record collection from memory. It was only when he realised that he needed to learn how to listen to what music was saying to him that a sense of hearing was partially restored, albeit accompanied by great physical pain and discomfort. So he concludes that he has had to develop a new way to listen, one that is active rather than passive.

One method of active listening, which Peter employs when trying to check something subtle but potentially troubling during a recording session, is to play a piece back whilst making a cuppa when not in full close up, focus mode. This synthesises the moment when someone hears your work for the first time and corrections can then be effected if there is, indeed, actually an issue. In a similar way there are songs that stand out on the radio as we are driving along - at times Peter has even stopped the car to catch who the artiste is (so annoying when the presenter doesn't say who?!) – and such times are examples of when a piece "speaks" to us, provoking us from a hearing only to a listening intently mode.

This endorses what Coleman concludes that hearing is passive whilst listening is deliberately active. It is therefore safe to propose, with Springsteen, that the more acute hearing of most musicians enables them to listen better than someone less musically gifted, and, when playing in an ensemble, engages that ability to promote special moments of making transcendent music together.

[3]
Play versus Plan

Why is it that the idea of play is so closely associated with the Arts? Musicians play their instruments and play together in groups. Artists play with paint while actors perform in plays and writers engage in word play. Most recently, a well known internet site for the sale of cds, dvds etc has been called play.com because that is what we do with their products. Pianist Alice Herz-Sommer has said that playing is her food and that, when she was allowed to play, it was like being in a service of divine worship. What is even more extraordinary is this thought was engendered whilst facing the most terrifying environment of captivity in a World War Two concentration camp.[31] What is there about the idea of play that it has become a word which is so fundamentally associated with the Arts? One aspect may be bound up with the improvisatory nature of play:

> There's a line in, I think, the New Testament,' U2's Bono told Joe Jackson of Hot Press before Zooropa was released, 'which says that the spirit moves and no one knows where it comes from or where it's going. It's like a wind. I've always felt that way about my faith. That's why on *Zooropa* I say I've got no religion. Because I believe that religion is the enemy of God.

> Because it denies the spontaneity of the spirit and the almost anarchistic nature of the spirit.[32]

He is talking of what Mike Campbell, lead guitarist in Tom Petty's Heartbreakers, describes as "bigger moments where spontaneous things happen". This embodies itself in lines such as "And I have no compass/And I have no map" from *Zooropa* and in U2's improvisatory approach to creating music and writing lyrics:

> On the road, U2 are constantly working informally on new ideas. As a matter of course, rehearsals and sound-checks are recorded. Frequently the germ of something new will emerge as the band improvise their way through a series of rhythm patterns and chord changes ... U2 songs often proceed along parallel tracks. On the one side, a set of musical ideas is taking shape. On the other, Bono and The Edge are developing bits of titles, lyrics, choruses and whatever other scraps of ideas have suggested themselves. The real heartache starts when they begin the process of bringing these different elements together.[33]

There would seem to be a correlation between this approach to music making and what is known of play theory in child development:

> During play children may begin by exploring and experimenting with what interests them by looking about, listening to and taking in the smells of their

home or early years setting, observing what goes on there and how the people in it behave. They may touch objects, move around the spaces, manipulate things, ask questions, as if they are seeking answers to the question 'What does this do?' This period of play and exploration has been called the epistemic phase (the gathering knowledge phase; Hutt et al., 1989) and it is typified by concentration and a serious facial expression. When children feel confident they have some knowledge they will move into a ludic phase of play (the fun phase), as if they are asking the question 'What can I do with this?' Both phases are equally important and link to Piaget's idea of assimilation and accommodation, where new knowledge is at first absorbed into and often understood in terms of previous knowledge. Then all relevant knowledge is adjusted as it becomes clear that the new knowledge has brought a different, challenging perspective that means the old knowledge needs expanding or correcting.[34]

Theologian and former Bishop of Durham, N. T. Wright has described Holy Scripture as being like a five act play containing the first four acts in full (i.e. 1. Creation, 2. Fall, 3. Israel, 4. Jesus).

> The writing of the New Testament ... would then form the first scene in the fifth act, and would

simultaneously give hints (Romans 8, 1 Corinthians 15, parts of the Apocalypse) of how the play is supposed to end ... The church would then live under the 'authority' of the extant story, being required to offer an improvisatory performance of the final act as it leads up to and anticipates the intended conclusion ... the task of Act 5 ... is to reflect on, draw out, and implement the *significance* of the first four Acts, more specifically, of Act 4 in the light of Acts 1-3 ... Faithful improvisation in the present time requires patient and careful puzzling over what has gone before, including the attempt to understand what the nature of the claims made in, and for, the fourth Act really amount to.[35]

Similarly, theologian Carl Ellis has written that, "Theology bears analogy with music in that it too can be approached as formal or dynamic".[36] Classical theology, he suggests, is concerned with "propositions" while Jazz theology is concerned with what happens when those propositions interact with pain, life and the moment. Ellis continues:

...God is not just classical. God is jazz. Not only does he have an eternal and unchanging purpose, but he is intimately involved with the difficulties of sparrows and slaves. Within the dynamic of his eternal will, he improvises. God's providential jazz liberates slaves and weeps over cities. Jazz can be robustly exultant or

> blue; God has been triumphant and also sad. Jazz portrays the diversity, freedom and eternal freshness of God. The genius of jazz theology is the theology as it is done.[37]

David Dark quotes Wynton Marsalis as saying that classical music is "harmony through harmony" and jazz as "harmony through conflict" in order to make a similar point. Such classifications can be disputed, not least on the extent to which dissonance features in twentieth century classical music, but, remaining with Dark's point for a moment, he suggests that:

> When we bring this way of putting the matter to the Bible, we find little in the way of classical music and plenty in the way of jazz, especially in the passages categorized as apocalyptic – whether it's trees clapping their hands, stars falling from the sky, bloody red moons, or crystal seas ... At it's best, jazz itself (with origins not unrelated to the bold imagination of the African-American church) gives voice to the groaning universe anticipating a new day. This is the business of apocalyptic.[38]

Just think John Coltrane or Albert Ayler for corroboration!

Like Wright, Ellis sees the Bible as providing the framework within which our improvisation can take place:

> Jazz theology is a participation in the basic patterns revealed in biblical life situations. It inquires not only what God did and said but how he said and did it. Furthermore, it expects him to do it again in a similar way in our lives ... Effective Black preachers respond to current situations by theologizing creatively on their feet, just as jazz musicians improvise new music and enliven old songs in response to the feeling and needs of the moment.[39]

Robert Gelinas writes:

> A Jazz Theologian is someone who knows that jazz is more than music. Therefore ... We are practicing Christians. We have spent time in the woodshed learning the old standards. Now we syncopate, improvise and respond to the call of a Love Supreme. We walk with Christ, embracing creative tension, joining in the mystery of life in concert. We have time, rather than time having us. We develop our ear so that we might listen to the needs of others, then live and love like Jesus. We live a composed life guided by the eternal melody of the Word of God as we add our own voice. We sing the blues so as not to waste any pain. We follow in the footsteps of our "kind of blue" Christ, offering our lives as statements to the renaissance that only He can bring. We have...found our groove! [40]

The closing section of one edition of BBC Radio 4's "Soul Music"[41] introduced Philip Sheppard, cellist and now composer. He spoke about how he was invited along to be part of the supporting orchestra for Elvis Costello's Meltdown Festival in 1995. One of the pieces was to be "Dido's Lament" which would be sung by charismatic rock singer Jeff Buckley. Although Philip had never heard of Jeff Buckley before, once he heard him singing it had a most profound effect on him:

> He seemed to screw every ounce of meaning out of the words and physically he looked like he was wracked with pain and anguish as he was singing it. But what was coming out was beyond ethereal his voice had this quality where it meant so much more than when I had ever heard it before... But then when he sang it seemed to be a lament so much more and it really went beyond what I would consider to be classical music ... and to date it's actually probably the greatest musical experience of my life, in as much as it turned my world inside out...

As a result Philip had to admit: "I know NOTHING about music - at all!"

> Up to that point I was a musician who played through study rather than a musician who played through feel and now I have to say I seek out people to work with

who do not necessarily read music who have their first sense is one of 'ear' rather than of 'technique'...

Philip then went on to say how this became a pivotal moment in his career which helped him to become a composer, enabling him to move away from being "a player who just repeated other people's music".

Jeff Buckley died in a tragic accident just two years later in 1997, subsequently his version of Leonard Cohen's 'Hallelujah' reached number one in the US Billboard charts and is considered by many to be the definitive version. Now Philip thinks of Jeff nearly every day and is ever grateful for the effect of the encounter, even though he only met him for around half an hour. On hearing this programme, Peter felt compelled to comment, "Listening to this has changed me, too".[42]

The sense that improvisory play gets the artist to a deeper level can also be found in the visual arts. Albert Herbert, for example, was an artist driven by a number of (artistically) unfashionable desires. He had a drive to make images and tell stories, to make accessible art, "paintings that are more public and easier to understand".[43] Coupled with these drives was a concern with revealing the inner world, the 'marvellous', feelings, and through these, the collective mind.

His reconciliation of these disparate drives involved learning to see and paint as children do - "I learned to draw again as if from the beginning, drawing what I felt and knew rather than what it looked like".[44] He also restricted himself to depictions of Biblical events and stories. These he treated as "symbols, metaphors, revealing the marvellous".[45] Religion he saw as revealing not just the inner world but also the collective mind.

His method of creating added a further level of reconciliation to his work. He explained that a painting usually started with some idea that could be put into words but that when he began to paint he became fully involved in "the struggle to harmonise shapes, colours and textures".[46] This could go on for several months with the original idea becoming lost in the paint only to re-emerge as something quite different. In this way he both drew his images from his subconscious and integrated them into the wholeness of the painting.

His approach tallies with that of another of his peers, Ken Kiff, who argued that his subconscious images only achieved meaning through the process of shaping and forming the painting. The painting, as a whole, had to be discovered, by the artist, bit by bit. This had to happen in order "for the thing to really grow together and be significantly all part of the same growing thing".[47] In this growth there could be a sense of peace, completeness and wholeness despite the presence, at times, of disturbing imagery.

Cecil Collins, too, came to use a similar approach to a united development of image and form. He called this process the Matrix. Collins' use of the Matrix involved the following; he would choose two complementary colours, then, with his eyes shut he would paint a number of brush strokes. He would then open his eyes and consider the marks on the paper or canvas. As he looked images would suggest themselves and he would select and paint the one that he wished to impose as the predominate image. The point of the Matrix was to "penetrate deeper into the creative imagination so that it is that which speaks to the artist and not the shallower levels of the mind ... The Matrix ... stands for all the hidden desires of the soul".[48]

These anecdotes also introduce the idea of play as discovery, an aspect highlighted by Michael Rosen in *Art Is Child's Play*, a BBC programme in the "Imagine" series:

> If you try to define play it's actually very hard because it's so diverse. But you can hear it in children when it moves from something very rule-governed from outside, when it starts moving to the rules that the children are making ... I always think of it as playing with trial and error, without fear of failure ... One of the great things about art is that it enables us to go exploring and retrieving things. But that sounds as if somehow or other it's totally conscious and the whole point is that sometimes it isn't and things pop up. That you don't know how or why they're there and then when you contemplate them, you discover things. So, one of the fundamental things about all art is the discovery process. You investigate and discover when you make things.[49]

This was brought home to Jonathan during the funeral service for his friend and fellow commission4mission artist, Peter Shorer.[50] Peter's son, Michael, spoke about the way in which his father taught him to solve problems:

> Dad was a great craftsman ... There seemed to be nothing that he couldn't make. Design problems were mere pebbles to be kicked aside en route to where he wanted to be. He started teaching me how to make jewellery when I was about 11 and always told me that if a problem seemed insurmountable, turn the whole thing upside down to get a different perspective. Hey presto, it works! He used this 'mantra' at the British Museum to great effect. As well as the incredible metalwork and ceramics he restored, was the solution to lifting an entire collapsed Roman wall plaster. He bonded the back of it to the same honeycomb structure that is used in the wings of Harrier jump jets. A few marine shackles, cables and levers later and it was upright. In fact, we have heard that when the keepers of departments came up against a seemingly impossible restoration, inevitably the phone would ring in Dad's workshop - "Shorer, could you spare a minute?"[51]

Turning things upside down G. K. Chesterton argues is a characteristic of mystics such as St. Francis of Assisi:

Francis, at the time ... when he disappeared into the prison or the dark cavern, underwent a reversal of a certain psychological kind ... The man who went into the cave was not the man who came out again ... He looked at the world as differently from other men as if he had come out of that dark hole walking on his hands ... Now it really is a fact that any scene such as a landscape can sometimes be more clearly and freshly seen if it is seen upside down ... Thus that inverted vision, so much more bright and quaint and arresting, does bear a certain resemblance to the world that a mystic like St. Francis sees every day.

This state can only be represented in symbol, but the symbol of inversion is true in another way. If a man saw the world upside down, with all its trees and towers hanging head downwards as in a pool, one effect would be to emphasise the idea of dependence. There is a Latin and literal connection; for the very word dependence only means hanging. It would make more vivid the Scriptural text which says that God had hanged the world upon nothing. ... he would be thankful to God for not dropping the whole cosmos like a vast crystal to be shattered into falling stars. ... the sense of a divine dependence ... for the saint is like the broad daylight.

... He who has seen the whole world hanging on a hair of the mercy of God has seen the truth; we might say the cold truth. He who has seen the vision of his city upside-down has seen it the right way up.[52]

Coming out of your cave walking on your hands is an image which Mumford and Sons use in their song *The Cave* to make the same point; when you see the world hanging upside down, you know the maker's hand in it all and understand dependence.

In biblical terms this sense of seeing the world from a totally new perspective - that seems to turn everything we thought we knew upside down, but, in fact, is seeing from the right way up - is expressed in 1 Corinthians 1: 18 - 25:

> For the message of the cross is foolishness to those who are perishing, but to us who are being saved it is the power of God. ... For since in the wisdom of God the world through its wisdom did not know him, God was pleased through the foolishness of what was preached to save those who believe. Jews demand miraculous signs and Greeks look for wisdom, but we preach Christ crucified, a stumbling block to Jews and foolishness to Gentiles, but to those whom God has called, both Jews and Greeks, Christ the power of God and the wisdom of God. For the foolishness of God is wiser than man's wisdom, and the weakness of God is stronger than man's strength.

Jesus, as Donald Kraybill has written in *The Upside Down Kingdom*[53], startles us as paradox, irony and surprise permeate his teachings flipping our expectations upside down: the least are the greatest; adults become like children; the religious miss the heavenly banquet; the immoral receive forgiveness and blessing. Things aren't like we think they should be. We're baffled and perplexed; uncertain whether to laugh or cry. Again and again, turning our world upside down, his kingdom surprises us and this is exemplified by the reversals of our expectations found in the Beatitudes.

Marc Chagall's inversions, metamorphoses and, defiances of gravity are, likewise, his attempt to depict, and to help us see, inner or spiritual realities. He has said that "to call everything that appears illogical, "fantasy", fairy tale, or chimera would be practically to admit to not understanding nature" and, "I've always been tempted by the supposedly illogical, invisible side of form and mind, without which external truth isn't complete for me". Accordingly, he states that "all our interior world is reality" and it is this that he paints. "What counts is art, painting, a kind of painting that is quite different from what everyone makes it out to be. But what kind? Will God or someone else give me the strength to breathe the breath of prayer and mourning into my paintings, the breath of prayer for redemption and resurrection?"[54]

Camille Bourniquel explains how such reversals of our expectations in Chagall's work enable us to discover more of reality:

The fantastic is the very essence and raison d'etre of the work. It is less a question of symbols than of an unveiled reality set before our eyes. Chagall knows that reason is often an obstacle to knowledge of the being and the world. This confusion of appearances that can perplex us carries us beyond the illusions that it creates before our eyes. The visionary does not hem himself in here in enigmas and phantasms. His creatures are not mere puppets or robots. These hybrid beings cannot be wound up like toys: they lead their own lives, are fragments of energy, symbols of the spirit which forever passes through matter and tricks logic. What counts here is not that donkeys fly, that roosters become gigantic canopies, that rabbis are green or red or blue like the seraphim in some apocalyptic vision, but that these infractions of natural laws, this illegality of form brings forth for us the light of the being in the heart of these mutations. The fantastic, or rather the imaginary, in Chagall's work is a form of knowledge, a gesture to embrace the world in its totality.[55]

[4]
Medium versus Message

We live in a culture that has been profoundly shaped by Christianity and yet where many people do not recognise those Christian influences or know the Christian stories. In such a culture how do you communicate Christianity? It is an issue that all believing artists face and two card carrying Christians who came up with interesting and, perhaps, surprising responses were the Catholic novelists, Flannery O'Connor and Walker Percy.

Flannery O'Connor wrote that:

> When you can assume your audience holds the same beliefs you do, you can relax a little and use more normal means of taking to it; when you have to assume that it does not, then you have to make your vision apparent by shock – to the hard of hearing you shout, and for the almost-blind you draw large and startling figures.[56]

The problem as O'Connor sees it is that non-believers do not recognise as sin those things that Christians view as sin. The whole concept of sin itself may be anathema to those who are not Christians and they may accept as completely normal things that Christians view as sinful. So she wrote that "the novelist with Christian concerns will find in modern life distortions which are repugnant to him, and his problem will be to make these appear as distortions to an audience which is used to seeing them as natural". In order to make things which seem normal to many appear as sinful to your audience you need to use the shock tactics of distortion and exaggeration, crisis and catastrophe.

Walker Percy writes about there being two stages in non-believing audiences becoming aware of grace. First, there is an experience of awakening in which a character in a novel (and through that character, the audience) sees the inadequacy of the life that he or she has been leading. This is a moment of epiphany or revelation about themselves; a moment in which they either realise their depravity or their potential for grace.

This is what O'Connor was talking about when she said that the job of the Christian novelist is to help the audience see activity that they regard as normal as a distortion. Such an experience may then lead on to the second stage of hearing and responding to the grace of God in Christ. What O'Connor and Percy both seem to suggest is that their characters and their audience cannot see the grace of God without the first stage of becoming aware of the inadequacy of their current lives.

There are many bands and singer-songwriters who have been influenced by the writings and ideas of O'Connor, Percy and others like them. T. Bone Burnett, one of these, got his first major break playing in the band for Bob Dylan's Rolling Thunder tour and has gone on to become a Grammy-winning producer (of the soundtrack to the film *O*

Brother, Where Art Thou?); an Oscar-nominated songwriter (for song 'The Scarlet Tide' from *Cold Mountain*); an indie record label founder; producer of albums for the likes of Elvis Costello, Roy Orbison, Tony Bennett, k.d. lang, Alison Krauss, Counting Crows, the Wallflowers, Sam Phillips, Gillian Welch, and Ralph Stanley; and a singer-songwriter himself who has released six critically acclaimed albums.

Burnett, also a Christian, provides us a profound quotation when he said that "if you believe Jesus is the Light of the World there are two kinds of song you can write – you can write songs about the light or about what you might see by the light".[57] His statement can provide a framework to help us look at different ways in which Christians have expressed their faith in and through popular music.

People can identify very deeply with songs. We see this in the way that people choose particular songs to mark major milestones in their lives (like weddings or funerals). We see it in the way that teenagers will play one song over and over and over again and we see it in the way that concerts can become corporate sing-alongs as the crowd knows all the words and takes over the singing from the band. We do this because there is something in the combination of the music and lyrics that connects deeply with what we are thinking and feeling at that time. When that connection is made the link can stay with us for a lifetime.

Great songs therefore are not propaganda or sermons, they are about empathy and making emotional or intellectual connections that reveal to us something about ourselves and our world. In other words, the best songs are like epiphanies; moments of revelation in ordinary life which reveal either the wonder or the depravity of life. Malcolm Guite has written of epiphanies as moments of transfigured vision:

> Sometimes ... the mirror of poetry does more than reflect what we have already seen. Sometimes that mirror becomes a window, a window into the mystery which is both in and beyond nature, a 'casement opening on perilous seas'. From that window sometimes shines a more than earthly that suddenly transforms, *transfigures* all the earthly things it falls upon. Through that window, when it is opened for us by the poet's art, we catch a glimpse of that 'Beauty always ancient always new', who made and kindled our imagination in the beginning and whose love draws us beyond the world.[58]

It is those moments of transfiguration, he writes, "those moments when the mirror a poem holds up becomes a window into the Divine," which are the subject of his book[59].

David Dark, by contrast, writes that:

> We apparently have the word "apocalypse" all wrong. In its root meaning, it's not about destruction or fortune-telling; it's about revealing. It's what James

Joyce calls an epiphany - the moment you realize that all your so-called love for the young lady, all your professions, all your dreams, and all your efforts to get her to notice you were the exercise of an unkind and obsessive vanity. It wasn't about her at all. It was all about you. The real world, within which you've lived and moved and had your being, has unveiled itself. It's starting to come to you. You aren't who you made yourself out to be. An apocalypse has just occurred, or a revelation, if you prefer.[60]

Two contrasting revelations both meeting the requirements for an epiphany. James Joyce set out the requirements or conditions for an epiphany in *Stephen Hero* (the early version of *A Portrait of the Artist as a Young Man*) where he writes:

By an epiphany he meant a sudden spiritual transformation, whether in the vulgarity of speech or of gesture or in a memorable phrase of the mind itself. He believed that it was for the man of letters to record these epiphanies with extreme care, seeing that they are the most delicate and evanescent of moments...
..."First, we recognize that the object is *one* integral thing, then we recognize that it is an organized composite structure, a *thing* in fact: finally, when the relation of the parts is exquisite, when the parts are adjusted to the special point, we recognize that it is *that* thing, which it is. Its soul, its 'whatness', leaps to

us from the vestment of its appearance. The soul of the commonest object, the structure of which is so adjusted, seems to us radiant. The object achieves its epiphany.[61]

This description of epiphany seems more aligned with Guite's sense of transfigured vision than it does of Dark's everyday apocalypse, although it is Dark who claims Joycean understanding. On the one hand this is because Joyce draws heavily on theology for his understanding of epiphany. He wrote, for instance, of the work that would become *Dubliners* as being "a series of epicleti". This term Terence Brown notes, "derives from the Greek Orthodox liturgy and refers to the moment in the sacrifice of the Mass when the bread and the wine are transformed by the Holy Ghost into the body and blood of Christ".[62] It is at this moment of consecration that "the everyday realities of bread and wine are charged with spiritual significance".[63] Similarly, the literal meaning of epiphany is manifestation but, in the Church calendar the Feast of Epiphany commemorates the manifestation of Christ's divinity to the Magi, colloquially known as the Wise Men.

Bernard Richards notes that with this definition Joyce "comes close to the aesthetics of Gerard Manley Hopkins and his philosophy of haeccitas ('thisness')". Richards also notes that, "For centuries writers and mystics have experienced sudden insights that seem detached from the flow of everyday perception". He cites William Wordsworth's *The Prelude* and Dante Gabriel Rossetti's

Sudden Light as examples, before stating that often these epiphanies "have been on a borderline between the secular and the religious: what has been revealed in the mystical moment has been a sense of God, of the whole shape of the universe, of the unity of all created things".[64]

On the other hand, Dark is right in stating that Joyce's use of epiphanies in his work was more to do with everyday apocalypse than with transfigured vision. Francesca Valente writes that:

> Joyce himself confirmed this in a letter of July 1904 to Curran, where he said that he intended Dubliners 'to betray the soul of that hemiplegia or paralysis which many consider a city' (Joyce, Letters 55). Joyce therefore conceived this work as a sequence of 'fifteen epiphanies' - as he stated in a letter dated February 8, 1903 to Stanislaus (Ellmann, James Joyce 125) - which were written to let Irish people take 'one good look at themselves in his nicely polished looking-glass' (Joyce, Letters 63-64). What emerges from these words is that both the fictional characters of the tales and the readers are meant to undergo an epiphanic confrontation.[65]

In the American South, there is a tradition of Appalachian country death songs; gothic backwoods ballads of mortality and disaster. Alternative rock band The Violent Femmes took that tradition and used it to confront their audience in 'Country Death song' with an epiphany of the reality, ugliness and consequences of sin. They told a story in which the central character acts in a way that all of us recognise as sinful and then spoke about the reality of hell as a consequence of what he that did. This song is, therefore, an example of what Flannery O'Conner was talking about when she wrote that "the novelist with Christian concerns will find in modern life distortions which are repugnant to him, and his problem will be to make these appear as distortions to an audience which is used to seeing them as natural".[66] In that situation she said, you have to make your vision apparent by shock and that is what the Violent Femmes did.

In her stories Flannery O'Connor also wrote about the way in which the holy interpenetrates this world and affects it. To refer to the Holy Bible again, St Paul in his letter to the Philippians, tells his readers to go through life with an attitude of looking out for things that are true, noble, right, pure, lovely and honourable. He expects us to find these things in our ordinary lives, if we look for them. Ohio-based band Over The Rhine sing in 'Jesus in New Orleans' that you never know just what on earth you'll find in the face of a stranger or in the dark and weary corners of a mind because, here and there, when you least expect it, you can see the Saviour's face. In their story of meeting a stranger in a bar in New Orleans in whose face and words they see something of Christ the holy is interpenetrating their world, and ours, and affecting it. In this way Over The Rhine created an epiphany that reveals Christ for us in the ordinary experiences of life.

Most forms of work do not exist primarily in order that people find out about Jesus. This is true whether we work in administration, construction, manufacturing, retail, service or some other form of work. It is also true of the music industry; it does not exist to help people see Christ, it exists to sell songs. Some Christians in the music business, as we have seen, find this a major problem.

Jerry Lee-Lewis and Al Green found irreconcilable differences between singing popular music and singing gospel music but T. Bone Burnett has already given us a different way forward. Christians don't only have to sing about finding the light of Christ. They can also sing about what you can see by the light of Christ; in other words what does life look like when you look at it from the perspective of a Christian?

To do this immediately changes the relationship between the singer and the audience. People who are singing to evangelise about the Light are preaching through song and telling their audience what to think or believe. People who are singing about what they can see by the Light are coming alongside their audiences and saying this is what life looks like to me, does that connect with you? It's a very different approach and relationship but it fits with the way in which people live with songs that make an emotional or intellectual connection with them. It is clearly no longer propaganda or preaching, so mainstream record companies can sell it, and it enables believing artists to ask questions that challenge people's contemporary lifestyles.

The Fly is a song by U2, found on *Achtung Baby*, which is written as a phone call from Hell, a description of the world as we know it - in darkness, the stars falling from the sky, the Universe exploded because of one man's lie. In this dark world we live in the middle of contradictions with much that we'd like to rearrange, although often all we achieve is to kill our inspiration and sing about the grief. In performance on the ZooTV tours U2 magnified these contradictions through the projection of aphorisms onto monitors, symbolising the overload of information we receive in an socially networked, media driven age. They challenged their audience to think about the possibility that everything they thought they knew might be wrong.

Their embrace of contradiction reflects our age and challenges it, at one and the same time. U2's idea was to use the energy of what's going against us - and by that they mean popular culture, commerce, science - to defend ourselves. Rather than resisting popular culture to try to walk through it rather than walk away from it. To describe the age, they claim, can be to challenge it. The job of artists, they have said, is to describe the problem, the contradictions, "to describe what's going on, describe the attraction, and be generous enough not to wave your finger at it as it's going by". U2 look for "diamonds in the dirt", shining, transcendent moments; sex and music as places where you glimpse God. They trawl through the state of confusion that is the contemporary moment - reflecting, mocking, embracing, describing - in order to glimpse God, resist or mock the devil and be a harbinger of grace. They try to cling to the face of love and shine like a burning star.

Bob Dylan converted to Christianity in the late '70s and, after releasing two albums that explicitly named the name of Jesus, he integrated his faith into his art by writing songs that view the world from an end times/apocalyptic perspective. 'Jokerman,' from the album *Infidels*, is a song depicting the apathy of humanity in the face of the apocalypse. We are the jokermen of the song's title who laugh, dance and fly but only in the dark of the night afraid to come into the revealing light of the Son of God.

The final verse comes straight from the Book of Revelation[67] and describes the birth of the Anti-Christ who will deceive humanity into following him rather than Christ. The accusation and challenge that Dylan puts to us in the final lines of this final verse is that, even though we know exactly what will happen (because it has all been prophesied in the Book of Revelation), we make no response; we are apathetic in the face of the apocalypse. Our lack of response is what is fatal to us because it is only through repentance and turning to Christ that we will be saved from the coming judgement. Without naming the name of Jesus, Dylan captures well the Biblical portrait of humanity as made in the image of God but marred by our rejection of God, with this perverting our potential for beauty and compassion into a selfish search for self-aggrandisement.

Johnny Cash sang openly about his faith and the strength it gave him, on songs like *The Beast In Me* from the first *American Recordings* album, but, as we have said, no one listening felt like they were being preached at. By singing about the reality of sin in his own life Johnny Cash enables us to think about the beast in our own lives. As a result, perhaps we too can pray as he does, "God help the beast in me".

Stonework's International Director Colin Harbinson has written that:

> God communicates by way of revelation. Christianity is a revealed faith. The scriptural understanding of revelation is "an uncovering" or "a showing." The content of revelation includes the uncovering or showing of "truth." For the artist this should come as both an encouragement and a challenge. Art works best when it shows rather than tells. Art is at its best when it uncovers what familiarity has concealed, and opens us up to a fresh perspective on truth – the truth about any subject. This would strongly suggest that artistic expression, at its best, is compatible with God's way of revealing truth to man. Both show, and both seek to show truth ...
> Jesus was the ultimate revelation; "the word made flesh." He alone could say, "He who has seen me has seen the Father." Incarnational reality is essential understanding for the artist. Art has the ability to "flesh out" or embody unseen or intangible ideas, thoughts, concepts, and worldviews ...

Jesus wanted people to search for the pearl of great price, so that when they found it, they would sell everything they had in order to obtain it. Our creative communication should be of such a nature that it requires something of its audience – asking questions – and allowing God to grant revelation to those who have ears to hear. The temptation to over-communicate in order that everyone will understand everything is a misguided notion. We must resist the tendency to give neatly packaged answers; it is not the Jesus style ...

In conclusion, art is at its best when it uncovers what familiarity has concealed. It makes the familiar appear unfamiliar, so that it can be revisited with fresh eyes. It is a shared experience as artist and audience meet. No room here for preaching or moralizing, but rather a powerful place of potential revelation as truth is uncovered and shown.[68]

Similarly in *Flickering Pixels*, which (amazingly, given the subject matter) is a very readable application of 'medium as message' insights from Marshall McLuhan and Neil Postman to Christian faith, author and church pastor Shane Hipps calls for the Church to lose the naivety of its relationship with media by developing awareness of the varying ways in which the mediums we use to express our messages affect the way in which those messages are received and understood.

Hipps argues the "gospel message is not a single abstract concept" instead it is "a story that changes and expands with each new set of characters and settings". We must remember, he suggests, that "the Bible is not merely - or even primarily - a collection of objective propositions" instead it is "a grand story told through hundreds of different perspectives and diverse social settings". As a result, its message is "multilayered, textured, expansive, and complex".[69]

The "print age led to an efficient gospel" where salvation "became as easy as 1-2-3: (1) believe in Jesus; (2) apologize for your sins; (3) go to heaven". In this way, "we were shown the power of personal relationship with Jesus" and "the heavily intellectual emphasis of the print age helped unlock the treasure chest of Paul's rich, rational, and nuanced theology".[70]

Now, "the image gospel is ... moving beyond cognitive propositions and linear formulas to embrace the power of story and intuition ... We move from understanding salvation as a light switch to seeing it as a gradual illumination ... The gospel is seen as a way of life that transforms the world here and now, not just in the next life".[71]

[5]
Chaos versus Connection

"A heap of broken images."[72]

This line from T. S. Eliot's *The Waste Land* could sum up the fragmentation of form and content in a poem which seeks to document the hopelessness and confusion of purpose in modern Western civilisation. Professor Randy Malamud writes that:

> *The Waste Land* is a series of fragmentary dramatic monologues and cultural quotations that crossfade into one another. Eliot believed that this style best represented the fragmentation of society, and his poem portrays a sterile world of panicky fears and barren lusts, and of human beings waiting for some sign or promise of redemption.[73]

The Velvet Underground, arguably one of the most influential bands in the history of alternative rock music, used dissonance – chaotic improvisations and bitter lyrics spliced to sweet melodies - in a similar way to Eliot's use of fragmentation. Lou Reed wrote in an unpublished essay from 1966, "New York filled with meaningless noises, which could be its redeeming grace".[74] Guitarist Lenny Kaye has said that:

If you want to write the story of the Velvet Underground, you have to begin far beyond any of the physical things that actually happened. You first have to look at New York City, the mother which spawned them, which gave them its inner fire, creating an umbilical attachment of emotion to a monstrous hulk of urban sprawl. You have to walk its streets, ride its subways, see it bustling and alive in the day, cold and haunted at night. And you have to love it, embrace and recognize its strange power, for there, if anywhere, will you find the roots.[75]

Music critic Nicholas Taylor sums up their mirroring in dissonant music of New York's meaningless noises which could be its redeeming grace, when he writes:

> Founded in New York, bred in New York, born of New York, the Velvet Underground, in their albeit brief existence from 1965 through 1970, explored the horrifying sins and the glorious salvations possible on the New York streets.[76]
> Sometimes we find ourselves on the edge, falling uncontrollably through life, punctured by a cannonball sized hole of despair, overwhelmed by emotion, facing the perhaps impossible task of trying to pick up the pieces and put ourselves back together from a pile of shattered fragments.

Glimpses of Clarity was an exhibition by George Triggs at the Art Academy which was featured in *art of England*.[77] *Broken* is the piece that provided the cover photo for this edition of the magazine and about which the above quote pertains. Triggs has written of this work:

> *Broken* goes about examining the fragility, isolation and silent determination of our existence. It captures the seemingly impossible task of picking up the pieces and putting ourselves back together after a complete emotional implosion. This life-size figure is in fractured pieces slumped on a stool. It is trying to rebuild itself, examining the deterioration of its own existence, examining what it means to be broken, questioning whether it can return to life anew, questioning whether the cracks and experiences stay below the surface and whether some pieces of itself are gone forever. *Broken* was created in solid clay, then cast as a hollow shell, which I then literally shattered into pieces and reassembled. Looking at all the pieces, it seemed like an impossible task, which made it both more exciting, exhausting and inspiring. The process was a huge emotional and thought-provoking journey for me which I feel transfers to the work.[78]

T. S. Eliot writes, at the end of *The Waste Land*, of shoring fragments against his ruin and that equates to Triggs' sculpture but both also capture a sense of the inspiration and revelation which comes as this shoring of fragments against our ruin takes place. Shoring up fragments against the ruins meant, to the extent to which he was able, to reconstruct. His seemingly disparate fragments include the Bible, the Grail legend, the 'Golden Bough', Tarot cards, Shakespeare, Dante, Buddha's Fire Sermon and many more. All were linked, reconciled, in the structure and content of a poem articulating a rejection of and movement away from the sterility of twentieth century life.

Welsh artist-poet David Jones regarded his poem *The Anathemata* as a series of fragments, fragmented bits, chance scraps really, of records of things, vestiges of sorts and kinds of disciplinae,[79] that had come his way by this channel or that influence. The poem was a collection of pieces of stuffs that happened to mean something to him and which he saw as "perhaps making a kind of coat of many colours, such as belonged to 'that dreamer' in the Hebrew myth." Jones celebrates not just the fragments themselves but the coat that they have been fashioned to form.

What Jones and Eliot did in constructing a whole from fragmentary materials is essentially similar to the form and construction of the Bible itself. Pastor and playright Mike Riddell, for example, has described the Bible as "a collection of bits" assembled to form God's "home page"[80] while Canon Mark Oakley uses a more poetic image when he speaks of the Bible as "the best example of a collage of God that we have".[81] Riddell and Oakley both develop their images of the Bible from the recognition that the whole Christian Bible contains, as Oakley says, "different views, experiences, beliefs and prayers" drawn "from disparate eras, cultures and authors" which are not systematic in their portrayal of God.

As Riddell states:

> The bits don't fit together very well – sometimes they even seem to be contradictory. Stories, poems, teachings, records, events and miracles rub up against each other. They come from all over the place, and span at least 4,000 years of history.

This is not surprising when there are four Gospels not one, when there are at least two different accounts of Paul's conversion and ministry, and when the principal form of the New Testament – the letter – is the form of long-distance, written conversation.

The Bible, then, does not move forward in the smooth linear style of, for example, a nineteenth century novel, an academic thesis, a sermon or a systematic theology. Reading the Bible in terms of linearity or chronology is a stop-start process involving multiple perspectives on the same key events or characters and extensive wastelands where little or nothing of significance happens or is recorded. We can learn about the Church in Ephesus, for example, from Acts, Ephesians, 1 Timothy, Revelation and, possibly, the Johannine letters but nowhere do we find a full, chronological telling of the story of that Church. The same can be said of all the Churches which Paul founded, including the Church at Corinth. The founding of this Church is recorded in Acts and the story then jumps to Paul's letters to this Church. These letters are a debate or conversation (not a story) between Paul and the members of the Corinthian Church about issues of concern to Paul and matters on which the Church had written to Paul for advice. We don't have the letters which Church members wrote to Paul or all the letters which Paul wrote to the Corinthian Church so the conversation as we have it is a little one-sided and incomplete, although we can infer some of the points made by the Church members from Paul's record of and response to them.

To ignore the disparate nature and form of the Christian Bible is to run significant risks as Riddell warns us:

> ... let us be aware that the assembled parts of the Bible are collected in a somewhat haphazard fashion. To push them into chronological order requires a great deal of scholarship, and runs the danger of doing violence to the material.

Yet, just as with Jones' and Eliot's work, Riddell and Oakley do not claim that the Bible is an entirely random collection. They both argue that the disparate materials are held together. Riddell says that, "what holds all these bits together is the fact that they somehow represent the continued involvement of God with the world in general and humanity in particular". Oakley suggests that "held together, they form a colourful and intriguing picture that draws us into its own landscape" and which enables Christians to "glimpse something of the divine being and his life in the world" and to find "a vocabulary for the Christian life".

The highly respected theologian Dr. Walter Brueggemann suggests that the Bible has both "a central direction and a rich diversity" which means "that not all parts will cohere or agree" although it has a "central agenda".[82] The Bible is, therefore, structured like a good conversation with a central thread but many topics and diversions. Brueggemann emphasises that "the Bible is not an "object" for us to study but *a partner with whom we may dialogue*". In the image of God, he says, "we are meant for the kind of dialogue in which we are each time nurtured and called into question by the dialogue partner". It is the task of Christian maturing, he argues, "to become more fully dialogical, to be more fully available to and responsive to the dialogue partner":

> ... the Bible is not a closed object but a dialogue partner whom we must address but who also takes us seriously. We may analyze, but we must also listen and expect to be addressed. We listen to have our identity given to us, our present way called into question, and our future promised to us.[83]

Playwright Dennis Potter's The Singing Detective presents a similar vision and one that can be linked to Jesus' restoration of Saint Peter following his denial (John 21. 15-

19). Just as Potter's central character, Philip Marlowe, cannot take up his bed and walk until he has reassembled the fragments of his past through memories, fiction and fantasy in order to confront the betrayals that lie therein, so Jesus makes Saint Peter confront his past and relive the experience of denial in order to move on from it into a future that is free of his past failures.

Leonard Cohen in his song "Anthem" highlights the sense in which we all are cracked and broken within our lives and that, it is actually through our cracked and fragmented natures that light comes into our lives and the world. He sings of ringing those bells which can still be rung, of forgetting our perfect offerings and acknowledging that it is through the cracks and flaws in our lives and creations that light – the divine – gets in.

This echoes 2 Corinthians 4: 6-12 in which Paul writes of our lives as being like cracked clay pots with the light of Christ shining through the cracks or fractures in our lives. Jonathan has reflected on this insight in the meditation that follows:

> Birthplace,
> least among the clans of Judea.
> Home town,
> a place from which no good was known to come.
> In appearance,
> without beauty or majesty, undesired.
> In life,
> despised and rejected, unrecognised and unesteemed.

In death,
made nothing.
His followers,
not wise, not influential, not noble – fools!

The light of the knowledge of the glory of God
in the bodies and form of human beings.
Light shining
through the gaps and cracks of clay pots.
Light shining
in the unexpected places, despised faces, hidden spaces.
Light shining
in the poor, the mourners, the meek, the hungry.
Light shining
in the merciful, the pure, the peacemakers.
Light shining
in the persecuted, the insulted, the falsely accused.
Light shining
in the lowly, the despised, the nonentities.
Light shining
in weakness and fear and trembling.
Light shining
in the foolish followers of the King of Fools.

The history of rock and roll is shot through with the kind of fragmentation we have been discussing because of the divide that is felt between the secular and sacred. But that is not the only way in which to think about these issues as there are artists who are saying that there are no splits and are bringing these unnecessarily divided concepts back together. They look towards the reconciliation of opposites, towards wholeness and affirmation, but recognise that, although we know of the existence of wholeness because of Christ, we are not yet whole ourselves. Like the characters in Flannery O'Connor's novels we are, at best, incomplete – even the good, she felt, has a grotesque face, because "in us the good is something under construction". One band who exemplify this approach to raising issues of faith in their music are U2.

In their songs, U2 celebrate the possibility of becoming one, of building a bridge between the sea and land, of coming home, of going where the streets have no name and, of believing in the Kingdom Come when all the colours will bleed into one. Theirs is a spirituality in which everything can be affirmed because everything can be transformed by grace. But they also affirm the ugliness and failure in our world, and in people like themselves. So, they sing of falling down, of being out of control, of losing their way in the shadows where boy meets man, of falling from the sheer face of love like a fly from a wall. In common with the Psalms, they mourn and rail at the pain and division experienced in the world - Ireland's bloody Sunday, El Salvador's bullets in the blue sky and Argentina's Mother's of the Disappeared.

In their hands these two poles are not opposed instead, both are embraced. U2's The Edge has said that: "We never did resolve the contradictions ... And probably never will. There's even more contradictions now ... but it's a contradiction I'm able to live with".[84] Contradictions that you are able to live with. This is where U2 take us - to an affirmation of both the goodness and fallen-ness of human beings. Into the still centre at the heart of the storm of contradiction to give a different take on reconciliation. Bono echoed the same theme in talking about their albums Achtung Baby and Zooropa:

> I decided that the only way was, instead of running away from the contradictions, I should run into them and wrap my arms around them and give 'em a big kiss.

'New Years Day', for example, suggests that although we are torn in two, we can be one. This is reconciliation in a lyric that - through images of separated lovers returning home and of a united crowd at a Solidarity rally - links public and private in the injunction to be one. War, the album from which 'New Years Day' comes, is, paradoxically, about surrender.

War was the outcome of internal conflicts between individual members of the band and the demands of their Christian faith, as they understood it at the time. Their reconciliation of these conflicts came, in part, from the understanding that Christianity did not divide body from spirit or sacred from secular. Instead these were, at best, reconciled and, at least, held together in tension.

Reconciliation is also embodied in their activism and working methods. U2 do not simply sing about the world's woes they also take practical actions to address them, whether this is contributing to concerts/records to raise charitable funds, symbolic actions such as their Sellafield protest for Greenpeace, or, most significantly, Bono's campaigning for debt relief through Jubilee 2000.

In their working method, scraps or fragments of music and lyrics are combined to create something that is larger than the sum of the parts. Their bass player Adam Clayton describes this as being "not just a playing thing - it's a whole supportive role within the commune".[85] Irish journalist John Waters has identified this sense of unity as a key feature in the impact of U2:

> As in no other band that I am aware of it, the music of U2 is a unity of all its parts. There is no sense that the music can be divided into its constituent elements - into voice, guitar, rhythm section, backing and accompaniment. It comes to you whole, maybe because that is the way it is imagined. The Edge plays the guitar, as Bono sings, Larry hits the drums or Adam plays the bass, not as an end in itself, but in order to serve the song. Voice and instruments are united in a single purpose: they tell the story.[86]

U2's spirituality, their language of reconciliation is not just about words - the lyrics are allusive containing hints and glimpses - but is also about the friendship between the four band members, their approach to composition and performance, the relationships and approach of their organisation. Their spirituality then, is a combination of words and actions and of on-stage and off-stage, characterised by movement, allusion, symbolism and action, aiming to express honesty, integrity and wholeness.

U2 are a group that emerged out of community. The four members met at Mount Temple, a non-denominational, co-educational comprehensive school in Dublin. Mount Temple aimed through education to cut across the traditional barriers within Irish society in a way that was genuinely radical when it opened in 1972. The personal backgrounds of the band members reflected the mix of communities across which Mount Temple was aiming to communicate. Mount Temple stands as a symbol of the reconciling and educative strands in U2's spirituality.

There were also other communities influencing the formation and development of the band members and their spirituality. Lypton Village was a gang of Dublin teenagers with a shared love of surreal humour, dadaism and boundary breaking through shock tactics. It was in this group that Bono and The Edge gained the names they have used ever since. Lypton Village is a symbol of U2's interest in contradiction, dramatic performance and subversion.

Then there was Shalom, a Charismatic house church[87], of which Bono, Edge and Mullen were members. Here there was an emphasis on exuberant worship and the direct inspiration of the Holy Spirit which included the manifestation of speaking in tongues[88]. In U2's past, Shalom symbolises the passion and improvisatory elements of U2's spirituality.

The impact of these communities was such that almost from day one many of the elements of U2's spirituality that we have been exploring were there in embryo. In a 1979 interview, given before they had signed a recording contract, Bono spoke about spirituality, improvisation, passion, humour, dramatic characterisation, failure and contradiction. In many respects, he could just as easily have been speaking in 1993 about ZooTV. That U2 could be speaking in these terms so early in their career demonstrates the impact of the communities of which they were a part in their formative period.

However, the most influential community has been the bond between the band itself. Where they have experienced conflict and tension within the band, this has generally been as a result of one or more members not sharing a particular community allegiance.

Throughout, their sense of community as a group has enabled them to work through the various tensions that have arisen at different stages within their career:

> It's a bit like joining the priesthood or the Mob. The only way you get out is when you die or when someone whacks you.[89]

These four communities – the barrier straddling education of Mount Temple, the barrier breaking dadaism of Lypton Village, the passion and spontaneity of Shalom's Christianity and the personal and committed friendships within the band - then stand as symbols of recurring elements within U2 that inform their spirituality.

Irish troubadour Van Morrison is another whose music is essentially reconciliatory. 'St Dominic's Preview' collects together memories of his childhood in Belfast, descriptions of his life in San Francisco, an all pervading sense of exile and unites them in a mystical centre – St Dominic's preview. His concern is to take the disparate elements of memory and experience and try to make the whole thing blend. At his best his songs are extended meditations that:

> Switch off what's referred to as the constant voice. That's what meditation is supposed to do - turn off the constant voice, all them thoughts you have, y'know, the refrigerator hum, did I leave the lights on? Or, is the dog crossing the street? What about my tax problems? When you switch off all that, that's what I mean by transcendence". He uses meditation and language in order to create; meditation "in order to pick up information", language in order to go back "trying to understand that you've arrived at a certain place and ... it's all biographical.[90]

Going back is a key phrase in Morrison's work. Going back into his past (how he has arrived at his current point of understanding), going back into Irish and Celtic traditions, going back to a world before rock 'n' roll and television where there was more silence and less rushing, more breathing and being together.[91]

Going back is where the healing comes from. In the present you are an exile, separated from the valuable things in life, from childhood visions, from community life, from silence, from closeness to God. Morrison's songs use melody, image, orchestration and vocalising to take us back to a point of silence, to a moment of communion, to a spiritual core. And it is fundamental that this comes about through a blending - not just of memories, visions, literature and songs - but also musically through a blending of blues, folk, jazz, gospel, r&b, soul and pop into a distinct style that transcends each individual genre. His art of reconciliation affects the whole of the work and is not solely concerned with content.

In 'Summertime in England' the orchestration and vocalising circles the song's core, ebbing and flowing with the movement between ecstasy and silence. Lyrically, we are on a journey from the Lake District through Bristol to Glastonbury picking up on the literary and spiritual references as we travel. We have a companion who could be a human partner or, to quote T S Eliot, "the third who walks always beside you".[92] Our journey ends, or begins afresh, in the Church of St John with a revelation of Jesus as the one who underpins spiritual life. "Can you feel the light in England?" Morrison asks. Have you felt it in Wordsworth, Coleridge, Eliot, Yeats? Have you felt it in memory, in landscape, in church, in drug induced visions, in the gospel music coming through the ether? And, as the music stills and the vocalising pauses, he asks us to touch the silence, the core of revelation. Don't touch, don't question, don't disturb, he pleads, just experience - it isn't about endlessly asking why, it just is.

Morrison's achievement in popular music is a unique one and while others have drawn on his musical synthesis for inspiration very few have been able to approach the wholeness of his approach. Singer-song writer Victoria Williams, however, is well worth singling out as one working along similar lines.

Williams has a naive, folky style which uses images and characters that would not be out of place in a painting by Chagall. This style, however, conceals a great subtlety of approach and a willingness to experiment with musical form in a similar fashion to that of Morrison. Williams builds songs that are not simply a melody running through verses and chorus but which, in tandem with the lyrics, veer off in directions that are consistent with the emotional ebb and flow of the song as a whole.

'Polish those Shoes' begins with children's counting games and contrasts childhood experiences of solitariness with those of family life. Reactions to both are mixed. Solitariness can come as the result of fears, family can be a place of overbearing discipline crushing exuberance. At the centre of the song is the contrast between parents expecting a spotless cleanliness from the children going to church and Jesus washing the feet of the disciples. The dominant approach taken by the parents contrasts unfavourably with the loving service of Jesus and results in the child's emotional, imaginative and spiritual development taking place outside of the home. The music conveys the exuberant bounce of the child, the subdued swirl of conflicting emotions as that exuberance is checked, and the quiet moment of revelation before building to climax with the vigour of the insistence on an imaginative life.

In Morrison and Williams, at their best, the whole thing - music, lyrics, vocal style, influences, memories, emotions, images, content - does blend to form songs that are more than the sum of their disparate parts. Songs that celebrate the reconciliation of their parts into a consistent and emotionally moving whole.

Artist Derek Hyatt writes that:

> Art is about modes of perception - how we see as much as what we see. We build up constantly changing models of the world from seemingly random thoughts and images. Artists seem able, with practice, to build this information into structures with meaning; they make things fit together.[93]

This occurs through "the gathering, the linking, the seeing, the shaping of different experiences into sequences within one picture".[94]

Such an art of reconciliation both mirrors and structures the workings of the mind, imagination and memory. David

Jones has graphically described, in the preface to *The Anathemata*, how this can take place in the work of an artist:

> The mental associations, liaisons, meanderings to and fro, 'ambivalences', asides, sprawl of the pattern, if pattern there is - these thought-trains ... have been as often as not initially set in motion, shunted or buffered into near sidings or off to far destinations, by some word or action, something seen or heard, during the liturgy. The speed of light, they say, is very rapid - but it is nothing to the agility of thought and its ability to twist and double on its tracks, penetrate recesses and generally nose about. You can go around the world and back again, in and out the meanders, down the history-paths, survey *religio* and *supersitio*, call back many yesterdays ... and a lot besides, during those few seconds taken by the presbyter to move from the Epistle to the Gospel side ... What I have written has no plan, or at least is not planned. If it has a shape it is chiefly that it returns to its beginning. It has themes and a theme even if it wanders far. If it has a unity it is that what goes before conditions what comes after and vice versa. Rather as in a long conversation between two friends, where one thing leads to another ....[95]

One writer who has developed the ideas that we have explored in this chapter into theories that are concerned not just with the arts but also with human development is novelist Nicholas Mosley. In *Catastrophe Practice*, the first of a series of novels bearing the same name, Mosley links the ideas of a variety of scientists, philosophers and artists - his "psycho-celestial football team" - in order to suggest that by observing patterns of thought and also the patterns of our ability to see (how we see as well as what we see) what we can "then be in contact with ... is a network of 'propositions, images, processes, natural pathology and what-have-you'; that is like 'some vast ecology or aesthetics of cosmic interaction': not only within the mind, but in connection with the world outside of which the mind is conscious: some circuitry going between, and around, these inside and outside worlds".[96]

Mosley describes his approach in terms that are strongly reminiscent of the linkages made by Jones, Chagall et al:

> Writers have been quoted by random selection here - Popper, Monod, Bateson, Young, Langer - random in that they were come across by this writer at least without plan but selected in that, it seemed, they were all connected by the same authority and liveliness and thus seemed to form, and not just in the writer's mind, their psycho-celestial football team. And this is the sort of occurrence that the writers themselves seem to describe - the way that out of activities of randomness there are formed structures as of a mind and by a mind: that such is life: all these writers in their different disciplines so unpremeditatedly but so

> luminously making connections - a state of affairs like Hermann Hesse's Glass Bead Game, the cosmic interaction of some World 3 Cup or like the conception and parturition of these plays [*Catastrophe Practice*]. Or like a molecule of DNA - the structuring and ordering of cells for survival - while most of the rest of the world - the world of running down, of entropy - goes its way.[97]

"This is the way", Mosley says, "in which the mind does work: consisting of connections, eliminations, selections: such processes being reflected in, and by, the world". "Beyond the cacophony there can be higher connections" and these connections are essential to survival. They can be described by "symbols of symbols: DNA, germ-cells, negative entropy, even divinities"! But the characteristics of those who embrace them remain similar:

> the ability to move between different levels of consciousness; the attempt at language capable of embracing seeming opposites from a higher point of view; the acceptance of errors as the purveyors of learning rather than traps; the becoming at home in such systems and codes of transformation.[98]

Mosley, thus, sees systems of reconciliation as a key to human development and survival. In his view art is a means of developing a language to see, think and speak in these terms.

The novelist Charles Williams - with his theory of co-inherence which he defines as "the recognition of the good, the exercise of intellect, the importance of interchange and a deliberate relation to the Centre"[99] - is another who has clear links to Mosley and his search for means of depicting goodness. Coinherence, for Williams, means the inseparability of flesh and spirit being inherent in creation and demonstrated to us in the incarnation. "By coinherence he means, of course, relationship; but he also includes mutuality, reciprocity, exchange".[100] His novels, therefore, in their style aim to be "inclusive in their scope" showing "control of a believed pattern of ideas" and creating an "illusion of simultaneity".[101] Content and technique reconciled. In the words of his character, Henry Lee:

> All things are held together by correspondence, image with image, movement with movement. Without that there could be no relation and therefore no truth. It is our business - especially yours and mine - to take up the power of relation.[102]

[6]

Head versus Heart

When Scottish singer Paolo Nutini sings that it was in love he was created and in love is how he hopes to die, he is equating love and creativity. The act of making love, he is saying, can also be an act of making in love. So, how can love and creativity interact and inform one another?

Making love (as opposed to casual sex) involves the union of opposites as a result of an attraction to one another born of mutual sharing. Love of the other as other grows from the sharing of enthusiasms, experiences, histories and interests and results in a coming together emotionally, physically and spirituality which creates a new partnership or family unit and, potentially, new life.

An equivalent for the artist to the love of another person could be a love of their materials, the tools of artistic creation; whether words, speech, sounds, paint, clay, stone, found objects etc. To love your materials may involve both an understanding of the way in which others have creatively used these same materials in the past (their histories) and an understanding through experimentation and use of their existing properties (their composition).

This is an idea and approach which would seem to have resonance with that of 'truth to materials', a phrase that emerged from the Arts and Crafts Movement through its rejection of the ornamentation of much design work (often

Victorian) which tended to disguise the natural properties of the materials used. The phrase has come to be particularly associated with sculptors and architects as both can reveal in their way of working and the finished article the quality and personality of their materials — wood showing its grain, metal its tensile strength, and stone its texture. Renowned sculptor Henry Moore, for example, wrote in *Unit One* that "Each material has its own individual qualities... Stone, for example, is hard and concentrated and should not be falsified to look like soft flesh... It should keep its hard tense stoniness".[103]

Nova Scotia's sculptor William E. deGarthe has spoken about how he 'releases' figures contained in a huge block of granite left in the backyard of his studio home when he moved there.[104] Similarly, Juginder Lamba is a contemporary sculptor for whom 'truth to materials' is significant and whose imagery (which is often faith-based) also explores loving creativity. Many of his works began with the artist searching through piles of joists and rafters looking for salvaged timber that would speak to him of its creative potentialities. His sculptures retain the personality and characteristics of the salvaged wood even at the same time as they are transformed into characters and forms of myth and metaphor. This sense of creative potential and possibility coming to birth is also expressed in the imagery of his works. The seed pod is a recurring symbol in Lamba's salvaged-work sculptures, seen as an image of creative power held in potential, and drawing on Tantric ideas of the union of male and female principles. Similarly, Lamba's sculptures *Conception* and *Birth* depict the womb as a wondrous container for the potential of a new life.

Sex and spirituality have been a potent combination for several modern artists. These include Eric Gill, Stanley Spencer and Marvin Gaye, where, in their private lives, the potency of sexual appetite overpowered spirituality in a destructive fashion and prevented the union of opposites which characterises Lamba's work. David Ritz, a biographer of Marvin Gaye, tells a story of working with Gaye on the original version of 'Sexual Healing'. This, in its original version, was a song crying out for healing from addiction to sex which, after Ritz's involvement had ended, was entirely reversed so that the song as released became a plea for healing through sex.

A more effective union of love and creativity can perhaps be found in the art of Marc Chagall. His painting *I and the Village,* for example, can be viewed as laying out the key parameter's for an art of reconciliation. In this painting an animal and a green faced man gaze lovingly into each others eyes as the man offers the animal a glowing branch that scatters light. Above them the green, yellow, blue and red houses of a Russian village turn onto their roofs while a man and woman move up the main street, the man upright, the woman upside down.

Here things and people are turned upside down, everything is in the foreground, and is alive, dramatic and moving. Chagall links up different, unusual and unlikely images in a way that makes visual and emotional sense and in a way that communicates his love of his home, his world, his people, its sights, sounds and smells. He succeeds, as Walther and Metzger have written, in "achieving a pictorial unity through the yoking of motifs taken from different realms of given reality".[105] He reconciles emotions, thoughts, reminiscences with lines, colours and shapes to create a harmonious, meaningful painting.

Colour and pattern emphasise the link between the large human face and the animal face. The eyes are linked by a line that cuts across the other diagonals. The tender green filling the human face highlights the loving gaze directed at the animal. Together they emphasise the emotional unity underlying the picture, that all these objects and images are loved by the painter. The images can be seen as bringing together four sections of creation; the human, the animal, plant life (the twig, bottom centre) and civilisation (the village). They bring together the strange (topsy turvey houses and people) with the ordinary (a man walking the village street, a woman milking a cow). They connect a person with a community, the 'I' of the title with the people and animals who populate the village.

These, together, may also hint at other unities; those of family where the animal may be symbolic of a mother figure, and the village, and all within it, caught up in a parent-child relationship. Or where the tender love expressed towards all these disparate objects is speaking of a spiritual unity with God expressed in every aspect of His creation and all linked and made worthy of love as a result. Whatever, Chagall has created a unity at every level within his painting so that both the medium and the content proclaim the possibility of reconciliation not solely within the confines of a frame but out there in the real world. If a human can reconcile within art, the painting seems to suggest, then reconciliation is possible within life as well.

We have seen then that the love and creativity encapsulated in human relationships can find equivalents within art in a love of materials and the union of opposites. However, there is also a sense in which love and creativity in art can move beyond the limits of human love into the infinity of divine love and this is captured well in a song by Victoria Williams entitled 'Lights'.[106]

The first verse equates creativity and life by asking what kind of song or life we wish to create. In both, the song suggests, we have a desire to create well – we want to make something good that will give lots of pleasure. But how will we react, Williams then asks, if our creation does not turn out as perfectly as we had planned? What if the thing we made wasn't quite perfect or there was something bad about it? Wouldn't we still love it just the same, still care about it, because it was our creation?

The refrain turns our attention to the lights of the city which look so good that it is almost as though somebody had thought they should. The lights of the city are designed by human beings who themselves are created by God. The lights of the city look good but the city is flawed because its human creators are flawed. There is something bad about the city and human beings as well as something good and yet God loves it and us just the same. To do this, to continue to care for a flawed creation shows divine love and is the example to which Williams calls us to pay attention for our own creativity through this song.

All this assumes, however, that art and music in particular are expressive of emotion; an idea which has, seemingly, been challenged by some composers. For instance, Stravinsky wrote in 1936 in his autobiography:

> For I consider that music is, by its very nature, essentially powerless to express anything at all, whether a feeling, an attitude of mind, a psychological mood, a phenomenon of nature, etc ... Expression has never been an inherent property of music ... It is simply an additional attribute which, by tacit and inveterate agreement, we have lent it, thrust upon it, as a label, a convention – in short, an aspect unconsciously or by force of habit, we have come to confuse with its essential being.[107]

However, in making this statement Stravinsky did not mean that music is not expressive, period, and he clarified what he actually meant much later, in 1962:

> The over-publicised bit about expression (or non-expression) was simply a way of saying that music is supra-personal and super-real, and as such, beyond verbal meanings and verbal descriptions. It was aimed against the notion that a piece of music is in reality a transcendental idea 'expressed in terms of' music, with the reductio ad absurdum implication that exact sets

of correlatives must exist between a composer's feelings and his notation. It was offhand and annoyingly incomplete, but even the stupider critics could have seen that it did not deny musical expressivity, but only the validity of a type of verbal statement about musical expressivity. I stand by the remark, incidentally, though today I would put it the other way around: music expresses itself.[108]

Commenting on these two statements in a *Guardian* article, jazz great Brad Mehldau comments:

> Stravinsky wanted to do away with a subtle but pervasive notion: that of a pre-existing idea or emotion that a composer will then set to music. A composer does not 'feel sad' and then write 'sad' music; that is a childishly reductive view of how music is created. It is the listener, after all, who assigns meaning, ideas and emotions to music once he or she hears it. We commit a blunder when we imagine a transcendental idea that existed before music, like one of Plato's ideal forms...
>
> When Stravinsky says 'music expresses itself', he is speaking of the process by which it comes into being – for himself at least. It does not borrow from language to generate itself; the composer does not have to have a particular feeling as he composes. Music's abstract quality – the way in which it does not refer to

something other than itself – gives it autonomy in this reasoning...

This is not cut and dried, of course. Someone could point to any number of works that seem to be driven by a specific idea, or music that we retrospectively know was inspired by specific feelings – happy, sad, what have you – that came about from an event in the composer or performer's life ... Stravinsky's statement was probably born out of frustration, as he repeatedly encountered reductive, mistaken characterisations of the composer's creative process. To the extent that he is correcting that reduction, I agree with him.[109]

Mehldau argues that a "musician does not necessarily need a wealth of experiences to express something that others will find profound" and gives, as examples, "Schubert's perfect song, Gretchen am Spinnrade" written when he was 17 and "Jimi Hendrix's album, *Are You Experienced*, recorded when he was 24":

> How was Schubert able to think up music like that - music that telegraphed the emotions of desire, fear, passion and unrest so uncannily? Doesn't it take wisdom to portray emotions like that? From where did young Schubert's psychological insight into female desire come? From what deep, sad place did a song like Hendrix's 'The Wind Cries Mary' emerge;

what informed the ecstasy of his Third Stone from the Sun - memories of high school?[110]

Mehldau's answer to these questions is that:

> Music is only representing wisdom for a group of listeners; it is not properly exuding it. So let us not assign this agency to music; let us more accurately say that the group of listeners is attaching a quality to the music - it comes from them.[111]

A similar discussion is sometimes advanced for the visual arts. So, for example, paintings of the crucifixion are nothing more than paint pushed around a surface to make marks that depict a man on a cross with any theological interpretation occurring in the viewer's mind not in the work. Yet these arguments seem too reductive, as there must be something in the work - music or painting - to which we can attach the emotion or theological interpretation. In other words, we do not attach the emotion 'sad' to any and every piece of music just as we will not interpret any and every painting theologically in terms of the crucifixion. This suggests that there must be something inherent in the music or the painting which allows or enables us to begin a dialogue with the work which includes our attaching a particular emotion or theological interpretation to it.

The question then becomes how to do this well. There seem to be at least five elements, which vary considerably in importance. The first and most important being an engagement with the work itself. A deep engagement with the work itself as a unified whole combining form and content is essential. Form and content cannot be separated, so it is vital to engage with and respond to the work as an integrated entity. Form and content inter-relate and their inter-relation must be perceived and appreciated if there is to be real engagement with the integrity of the work. All interpretation must therefore begin with and constantly relate back to the unique combination of form and content which is the work itself.

The unified whole that is the work exists in relation to the artist who created it as a child exists in relation to her/his parents. The child is always a person in his/her own right who can be known and encountered entirely independently of the parents yet who has been formed by both the genes and upbringing of the parents and continues to be, whether in revolt against or in harmony with, in relationship with her/his parents. Similarly, an artwork can never be defined by the intent or history of the artist that created it but both the artist's intent and history can shed valid and valuable light on the work.

Each work also exists within a range of different contexts. The most obvious is the physical context of the space in which it is encountered; the concert hall or gallery, for example. The inter-relation between the space and the work is most explicit in site-specific works but is a factor in response to all works. Other contexts include the social and cultural time in which it has been created, whether or not the work specifically refers to aspects of these or not (just as a child can be in revolt against or in harmony with his/her parents, so an artwork may respond to or react against its social and cultural context), and its place within the history of its genre and movements within that genre (again, rejection or assimilation may be involved) including the influence of other art upon its creation and the effect that its creation has on the history and movements within its genre. Furthermore each work also generates its own critical trail as it is reviewed, analysed, interpreted and categorised by conductors, critics, curators, historians and other artists.

Finally, each viewer makes their own personal response to the work. One that is inevitably influenced by the factors already listed but which always holds the potential, because of the unique combination of influences and perspectives that each viewer brings, to perceptions which may differ markedly from those generated by these same factors.

Contemplation and reflection are key if the varied nuances of each work are to be perceived and integrated. Often the time required is not given affecting the quality and integrity, our own very much included, of the interpretation.

An example of responses to a piece of music varying depending on the context in which it is played is found with the excerpt of Sir Edward Elgar's 'Nimrod' from the Enigma Variations that is invariably played at solemn events, including Remembrance Day. Whilst the whole 9th variation is about Elgar's friendship with one Augustus J. Jaeger and is, in part, relatively exuberant, the 2nd part illustrates some encouragement Jaeger offered to keep Elgar composing during which Jaeger used Beethoven as an example to inspire Elgar. However, when 'Nimrod' was played at Winston Churchill's funeral in 1965 the piece was effectively hijacked to represent something more weighty and sombre. However, sometimes various elements of performance, players and the event itself can transcend such a subsequent adoption.

This phenomenon occurred dramatically at London's South Bank Centre in 2012 during a return visit of the celebrated musicians of the Simón Bolívar Symphony Orchestra of Venezuela along with their charismatic conductor Gustavo Dudamel.

Whilst much has been written about the Venezuelan initiative, El Sistema, which encourages youngsters as young as three years old to be part of a disciplined community that learns to play classical and traditional musical instruments, nothing quite prepares you for experiencing them in real life

It is an aural and visual feast; inspiring, encouraging and profoundly moving. In interviews Gustavo Dudamel stresses the community aspect of El Sistema yet it is abundantly clear the combination of his enthusiasm and humility along with the vision of founder Maestro José Antonio Abreu are also key elements to this success story.

During one concert the orchestra enchanted a captivated audience with a sophisticated program of Beethoven, the players swirling in a hypnotising synchronicity with the music. After taking many bows Gustavo picked up the microphone to announce they would play one more piece 'because we love it', adding 'and we love you'. This encore was 'Nimrod', a sublime rendition transcending any thoughts of associations to Winston Churchill's funeral or even the composer's original homage to his friend Jeager.

A Classic FM radio presenter in attendance was moved to say, 'that was the most electrifying performance of Nimrod I have ever heard in my life'. But it was happened next that really set it apart. As the final E^b chord faded, Gustavo reverentially moved his baton down and closed his eyes. There then ensued a most sacred, pin drop silence that lasted for a full 28 seconds. The El Sistema community now had extended to everyone in the auditorium, all became one. Gustavo opened his eyes, smiled at his players, the moment passed and the audience burst into a rapturous ovation. A glimpse of the divine, perhaps, who probably said, "well done my good and faithful servants, that was very good!".

[7]
Search versus Stasis

Music moves; big band music swings, brass bands march to the beat of drums, while classical music is often structured by movements.

In some cases the sense of movement we find appears in the content of songs and across an artist's career. Bob Dylan, for example, comes from the tradition of hobo[112] singers (such as Woody Guthrie) and beat poets (like Jack Kerouac)[113] for whom the journey and the documenting of their experience is life itself. Dylan as journeyman, as traveller, is the key insight of the liner notes for *Tell Tale Signs* where writer Larry Sloman signs off with a paragraph quoting a myriad of phrases inspired by Dylan's lyrics:

> He ain't talking, but he's still walking, heart burning, still yearning. He's trampling through the mud, through the blistering sun, getting damp from the misty rain. He's got his top hat on, ambling along with his cane, stopping to watch all the young men and young women in their bright-coloured clothes cavorting in the park. Despite all the grief and devastation he's seen on his odyssey, his heart isn't weary, it's light and free, bursting all over with affection for all those who sailed with him. Deep down he knows that his loyal and much-loved

companions approve of him and share his code. And it's dawn now, the sun beginning to shine down on him and his heart is still in the Highlands, over those hills, far away. But there's a way to get there and if anyone can, he'll figure it out. And in the meantime, he's already there in his mind. That mind decidedly out of time. And we're all that much richer for his journey.[114]

Dylan's manifesto for his work is 'A Hard Rain's A-Gonna Fall'; a song about walking through a world which is surreal and unjust and singing what he sees - a newly born baby surrounded by wolves all around it, a road made of diamonds with nobody using it, a dark branch from which blood persistently drips, a room full of men who bloodied hammers.

This is a song which has been interpreted as dealing with events that were contemporary to the time (early 1960s) such as the Cuban missile crisis and, more generally, the threat of a nuclear holocaust. That maybe so, but a more straightforward interpretation and one that is closer to what the lyrics actually say is to see it as a statement by Dylan of what he is trying to do in and through his work. In the song he walks through a surreal and unjust world, ahead of him he sees a gathering apocalyptic storm and he resolves to walk in the shadow of the storm and sing out what he sees.

This then is the other key element to Dylan's journey and work; the idea of journeying in the face of the coming apocalypse. What we have in the best of Dylan is a contemporary Pilgrim, Dante or Rimbaud on a compassionate journey, undertaken in the eye of the Apocalypse, to stand with the damned at the heart of the darkness that is twentieth century culture.

Songs like 'When The Ship Comes In' and 'The Times They Are A-Changin' both deal with rapidly approaching change described in apocalyptic terms. When the apocalyptic moment arrives, it is clear that some will be on the positive side of the change and others not. Dylan may well be speaking, as has been suggested by many critics, about young versus old and freedom versus rules but, on the basis of the lyrics themselves, it is not possible to be definitive because the language Dylan uses is deliberately unspecific. In neither song does he identify the specific nature of the change that is to come and it is this generality which gives these songs universality and continuing relevance because they can be applied to different circumstances at different times. What can definitively be said about both songs however is that they are warnings about a coming apocalyptic change and the warning is to do with which side of that change we will be on.

From 'Slow Train Coming' onwards Dylan equated the apocalypse with the imminent return of Christ (also known as the Second Coming). The return of Christ in judgement is the slow train that is coming around the bend and in the face of this apocalypse he calls on human beings to wake up and strengthen the things that remain. Similarly, in 'The Groom's Still Waiting at the Altar', he sees the apocalypse coming as a curtain which is rising on a new age but not yet here, while the Groom (Christ who awaits his bride, the Church) is still waiting at the altar. In the time that remains he again calls on human beings to arise from our slumber ('Dead Man, Dead Man'). In the light of this thread in Dylan's songs throughout this period, it also seems consistent, as we have seen, to read 'Jokerman', from Infidels as another song in this vein; a song depicting the apathy of humanity in the face of the apocalypse and one which is shot through with apocalyptic imagery drawn from the Book of Revelation.

For much of his career, while consistently writing in the face of a coming apocalypse, Dylan did not specifically equate that apocalypse with the imminent return of Christ. Apocalyptic change in Dylan's work can be understood as generational conflict, Cold War conflicts, nuclear holocaust, Civil Rights struggles, and more. The generic message throughout is that apocalyptic change is coming and we need to think where we stand in relation to it. That message is as relevant today in terms of economic meltdown, climate change or peak oil, as to the Second Coming, whether imminent or not.

Dylan's songs document where his pilgrim journey in the eye of the apocalypse had taken him. He travels the paths of political protest, urban surrealism, country contentment, gospel conversion and world weary blues. On his journey he: sees seven breezes blowing around the cabin door where victims despair ('Ballad of Hollis Brown'); sees lightning flashing for those who are confused, accused and misused ('Chimes of Freedom'); surveys 'Desolation Road'; talks truth with a thief as the wind begins to howl ('All Along the Watchtower'); takes shelter from a woman ('Shelter from the Storm'); feels the idiot wind blowing through the buttons on his coat, recognises himself as an idiot and feels sorry ('Idiot Wind'); finds a pathway to the stars and can't believe he's survived ('Where Are You Tonight? Journey Through Deep Heat'); rides the slow train up around the bend ('Slow Train'); is driven out of town into the driving rain because of belief ('I Believe in You'); hears the ancient footsteps join him on his path ('Every Grain of Sand'); feels the Caribbean Winds, fanning desire, bringing him nearer to the fire ('Caribbean Wind'); betrays his commitment, feels the breath of the storm and goes searching for his first love ('Tight Connection to My Heart'); then at the final moment, it's not quite dark yet but he's walking through the middle of nowhere trying to get to heaven before the door is closed ('Tryin' To Get To Heaven').

In other instances, a sense of movement can be found within a single work such as Estonian composer Arvo Pärt's 'Credo'. This is music which takes the listener on an emotional faith journey beginning with a confident fanfare of belief but then descending into the dissonant chaos of doubt before emerging into a more hesitant state of trust which opens out into contemplative silence. This is music to pray along with as you inhabit the emotional states conjured by this composition. Jonathan has written a meditation which seeks to mirror the emotional journey conjured up by Pärt's music:

1
We believe
and the world is changed
around us
like the sun rising
over far-off hills
bringing the dawn.
We believe
and are enveloped
in the warmth
of acceptance and love.
We believe
and find a firm foundation
unshaken
and unshakeable.
We believe
and build
with gold
and precious jewels.
Called, selected, trained,
commissioned and ordained
we are the messengers of God.
His servants and the shepherds of his flock.
Pastor, teacher, leader,
prophet, priest and preacher.
We are servants of Christ,

stewards of his revelation
and parents in his family.
2.
We believe
and are stretched
taut, like a band,
between
all that we and the world
could be and are.
We believe
not knowing whether
we shall be released and fly
straight and true
to the future Kingdom coming
or snap,
in the present,
in two.
Overwhelmed by work and needs,
confused by scandals and controversies,
frustrated by structures and procedures,
defeated by our failures and inadequacies.
Whirled by the speed of change,
uncertain of our impact,
unnerved by decline,
unsure of our leaders
and ourselves.

In the valley of the shadow,
the dark night of the soul
where tormenting mind torments yet,
the hurt nerves whine
and we reach for the whiskey,
in the done darkness where we lie
wrestling with God,
our friend become our enemy,
and wake to feel the fell of dark,
not day.

3.

We believe
through the valley of the shadow
through the inadequate
through isolation.
We believe
through conflicting interpretations
through varying shades of grey
through manipulation
We believe
through labelling and stereotyping
through compromise and disillusion
through exhaustion
We believe
being both empty and full
being unknown and known
being unknowing and knowing.

We are Saul and Paul,
Simon and Peter,
Martha and Mary.
We are brothers and sisters
of those 'Son's of Thunder'.
We are in conversation
with ourselves,
each other,
our Church and churches,
and with God
who listens, argues,
changes his mind,
takes our part
and undermines us,
sets us at rest
and takes us
through the valley
of the shadow of death.
In the dialogue
we find ourselves,
we find each other,
we find mission,
adventure,
challenge,
change
and love.

We find
God.

Tarkovsky has written of chaos or crisis as the stimulus for movement:

> A spiritual crisis is an attempt to find oneself, to acquire new faith. It is the apportioned lot of everyone whose objectives are on the spiritual plane. And how could it be otherwise when the soul yearns for harmony, and life is full of discordance. This dichotomy is the stimulus for movement, the source at once of our pain and of our hope: confirmation of our spiritual depth and potential.[115]

Tarkovsky also suggests that this dichotomy which stimulates movement is also a key part of the creative process itself:

> Hideousness and beauty are contained within each other. This prodigious paradox, in all its absurdity, leavens life itself, and in art makes that wholeness in which harmony and tension are unified. The image makes palpable a unity in which manifold different elements are contiguous and reach over into each other.[116]

However, movement is not an end in itself and, as the composer Roxanna Panufnik has noted in some beautiful reflections on the music of Arvo Pärt, the beauty in spirituality can lie in just "'being" – stillness, meditative blankets of slowly shifting harmonies and letting the reverberant acoustic of churches and cathedrals do the work".[117]

Pärt's work, along with that of John Tavener and Henryk Górecki, has been labelled 'holy minimalism' and "has found an enormously receptive audience, filling concert halls and generating best-selling CDs by reuniting classical music with, of all things, contemplative spirituality"...[118]:

> The popularity of Tavener, Pärt and Górecki is interesting because they reject values typically associated with contemporary classical music. "Holy minimalism" is to music what contemplative spirituality is to prayer. To most of us, prayer involves addressing our words to God; but to the contemplative, prayer means listening in receptive silence. Whereas in traditional classical music you expect to hear development of musical ideas moving forward to a climactic conclusion, *this* music seems to go nowhere - and that is intentional. The purpose is contemplation. The music is meditative, hypnotic, and gently repetitive, as in the Christian tradition of centering prayer one might continuously repeat a word or two from Scripture to be drawn deeper into prayer. The gentle repetition gives the music a feeling of stasis, of being suspended in time. "Time and

timelessness are connected," wrote Pärt. "This instant and eternity are struggling within us. And this is the cause of all our contradictions, our obstinacy, our narrow-mindedness, our faith and our grief".[119]

Professional singer Martha Ainsworth tells a story which sums up the resolution between search and stasis pioneered by Tavener, Pärt and Górecki:

> "The silence must be longer", I protested. "This music is about the silence. The sounds are there to surround the silence."[120]
>
> The conductor, rehearsing *The Beatitudes* by Arvo Pärt, looked skeptical. He sought a rational analysis. "Exactly how many beats?" he demanded. "What do you do during the silence?"...
>
> "You don't *do* anything", I explained, "you wait. *God* does it."[121]

Similarly, Scottish composer James Macmillan wrote of John Cage:

> The interesting thing about Cage, with his aesthetics of silence, noise and music, was that his most famous or notorious piece, 4'33", which is 4 minutes 33 seconds of silence — a kind of rhetorical gimmick, but a real challenge to the culture in many other ways — was originally entitled *Silent Prayer*.[122]

[C]
In Conclusion

On 15th September 2001 conductor Leonard Slatkin led the BBC Orchestra in a dramatic rendition of Samuel Barber's Adagio for Strings at the BBC Proms. This was a change added to the usual program of jingoistic ditties that is regularly played at the Last Night of The Proms. Some questions readily arise:

1. Was it the proximity to the tragedy of 9/11 that made it so spine tingling?
2. Does the music carry such gravitas in itself that has made it one of the most popular classical pieces?
3. Was it because the Proms broke with traditions, held since inception, to invite a USA citizen to conduct the Last Night?
4. Was it the interpretation that Leonard Slatkin brought to the piece being an American and therefore relating more strongly to 9/11?

Furthermore, are we prepared to embrace the notion that Barber, when composing his Opus 11, sensed that this moment would arrive, when, one day, his piece would become a majestic incarnation, even though he would have clearly been unaware of the detail and extent it would be able to provide such succour to body, soul and spirit years later? In summary, was the music itself 'prophetic'?

It is safe to assume that being present in the Royal Albert Hall at the time with the additional ambience and audio dynamics was definitely preferable to the somewhat diluted intensity of viewing on TV. Regardless, many watched transfixed, sharing this special moment simultaneously, yet this remote experience was both tempered by production decisions and would have potentially been instantly spoiled by a disturbance such as a telephone call. Watching on video now does not provoke the same intense response, it certainly triggers recall, but it is not of the moment. However, sometimes the corollary may apply as we consider whether some performances take on greater significance after the actual event as time passes as the cache builds from word of mouth, a reflection of the earlier oral traditions?

This was not an aggressive response, but a truly spiritual one, with everyone experiencing something of God through the pain and suffering. Other examples might include the moment during Live Aid in 1985 when the CBC video of Ethiopian famine victims had been cut to 'Drive' by The Cars or the international Beatlemania phenomena.

Billy Bragg provides a further example in his book *The Progressive Patriot*:

> I realized early on in my career that responsibility for changing the world lies not with the performer but the

audience ... What a performer *can* do, however, is to bring people together for a specific cause, to raise money or consciousness, to focus support and facilitate an expression of solidarity. Which is precisely what The Clash did in Victoria Park for Rock Against Racism. Before I saw the hundred thousand like-minded souls gathered that day, I was reluctant to oppose the casual racism I'd heard at work. The realization that I was not the only person who hated what the NF stood for gave me the courage to speak out against the racists and homophobes...

The Clash taught me a valuable lesson that day, which I have in the back of my mind every time I write a song or step out on to a stage: although you can't change the world by singing songs and doing gigs, the things you say and the actions you take can change the perceptions of members of the audience. The Clash brought me to RAR, Tom Robinson introduced me to the politics of sexuality, and those brave gay men with their big pink banner made me realize that we were all on the same side. And although the world was just the same as it had always been as I travelled home on the Tube that evening, my view of it had been changed for ever.[123]

All of the above plus much more constitute elements of a 'coincidence' and this is actually 'The Secret Chord' with its unique properties encompassing all aspects of that special moment. It is what Tarkovsky said of the image; a making palpable of "a unity in which manifold different elements are contiguous and reach over into each other". It is art, he wrote, which "makes that wholeness in which harmony and tension are unified":

> It is no accident that in the course of nearly two thousand years of Christianity, art developed for a very long time in the context of religious ideas and goals. Its very existence kept alive in discordant humanity the idea of harmony... Art embodied an ideal; it was an example of perfect balance between moral and material principles, a demonstration of the fact that such a balance is not a myth existing only in the realm of ideology, but something that can be realised within the dimensions of the phenomenal world. Art expressed man's need of harmony and his readiness to do battle with himself, within his own personality for the sake of achieving the equilibrium for which he longed.[124]

The Secret Chord is a recognition of 'coinherence' (the coming together of things) and 'coincidence' (the unexpected coming together of things in a providential way). Recognising and welcoming these coincidences is a means of keeping "in step with the Holy Spirit".[125] Scott Peck calls this the "principle of synchronicity" and views it as an expression of God's grace.[126] In their song entitled 'Synchronicity', the Police describe this phenomenon as almost imperceptible and inexpressible, a connecting principle which is linked to the invisible. If we share this sense of synchronicity then we are able to dream Spiritus mundi (Spirit of the world – a sense of the interconnection of all things).

Arthur Sullivan described well the unexpected nature of The Secret Chord in his somewhat prosaic yet intriguing 1877 song 'The Lost Chord'. The lyric describes Sullivan's fingers idly wandering over a noisy church organ not knowing what he was playing until he strikes a chord which sounds like a great 'Amen'. The sound of this chord flooded the twilight with a sound like the end of an angel's psalm and calmed the composer's fevered spirit.

The song concludes by noting the transient nature of the Lost Chord, in vain he continues to seek this one divine sounding chord and concludes that he may only experience it once more in heaven 'spoken' by an angel!

Interestingly Jesus Christ's teaching about time is never concerned with abstract clock time ('chronos', a word he doesn't ever use) instead he speaks of 'kairos', time as opportunity, the opening up of the succession of historical events so that something can happen – in this instance so that the Secret Chord can be found. There is no record in the Gospels of Jesus having anything specific to say about music and, apart from the singing of psalms on the way from the Last Supper to Gethsemane, there is no biblical record of him as a musician himself. Yet the pre-Christian meaning of the word kairos (on which Jesus may well have drawn) refers to the art of oratory: how you communicate with an audience. So it may be that Jesus' own use of the Secret Chord was in his preaching, which gripped and amazed people with its beautiful lyricism and improvisations on scriptural themes.[127]

In the Oscar winning film *Chariots of Fire*, devout Scottish Christian athlete Eric Liddell says, "[God] made me fast, and when I run, I feel His pleasure." It is in those unrepeatable moments in history in which it all comes together.

It is therefore possible to conclude that The Secret Chord constitutes elements both encompassing and being part of a performance, an unrepeatable event in history, a moment in time, in which harmonies echoing from our discordant lives link all perplexèd meanings into one perfect peace where we feel God's pleasure. The Secret Chord, as Leonard Cohen stated, is indeed pleasing to the LORD.

[NB]

Notes and Bibliography

All hyperlinks and more information on:
www.thesecretchord.co.uk

[1] A cover version is a song sung as an alternative version not considered the original or a version not by the author and composer. http://en.wikipedia.org/wiki/Cover_version

[2] From the Old Testament reference: 1 Samuel 16:14-23 http://www.biblegateway.com/passage/?search=1%20Samuel%2016:14-23&version=NIV

[3] This is capitalised to be in line with translations of the Bible where the word 'God' has many different spellings in the original.

[4] A rectangle of proportions found frequently in nature that replicates itself when folded over on itself.

[5] Where a group of musicians play in an unscripted, impromptu fashion, making music together instinctively.

[6] http://en.wikipedia.org/wiki/Million_Dollar_Quartet

[7] Pentecostalism arrived in the American South following the post-Civil War holiness revival and was characterised by believers speaking in unknown tongues, worship in free-form churches, and the breaking down of social barriers that had long divided traditional Protestants.

[8] http://en.wikipedia.org/wiki/Jerry_Lee_Lewis

[9] I. Hoare ed., *The Soul Book*, Methuen, 1975.

[10] L. Barton, *Hail, Hail, Rock 'n' Roll*, The Guardian, Thursday 21 July 2011.

[11] To turn around and move in a different direction.

[12] B. Flanaghan, *Written In My Soul*, Omnibus Press, 1990.

[13] N. Hentoff, The *Playboy* Interview in C. McGregor ed. *Bob Dylan: a retrospective*, Angus & Robertson (Publishers) Pty Ltd, 1973.

[14] G. Marcus, liner notes to *The Basement Tapes* by Bob Dylan & The Band, Columbia, 1975.

[15] B. Flanaghan, *Written In My Soul*, Omnibus Press, 1990.

[16] http://www1.salvationarmy.org/heritage.nsf/0/42d53ced9ec1583080256954004bff3e?OpenDocument

[17] Transcribed from quotes by both Nickey Gumbel (Alpha Course recordings) and Shane Hipps

[18] D. Adam, *Power Lines: Celtic Prayers about Work*, SPCK, 1992.

[19] http://www.prweb.com/releases/2012/8/prweb9806603.htm

[20] G. Greig, Sting: *The X Factor kids are going nowhere*, Evening Standard, 11.11.09.

[21] *Sculpting In Time*, University of Texas Press, 1986.

[22] Ibid.

[23] http://banksyboy.blogspot.co.uk/2010/02/why-modern-worship-songs-are-crap.html attributed to musician Julie Hall.

[24] N. Page, Authentic, 2004.

[25] A reference to Jesus' action to clear traders and money changers from the Temple in Jerusalem. The Temple should have been a house of prayer but had become a hideout for thieves.

[26] Ibid.

[27] http://commissionformission.blogspot.co.uk/

[28] http://www.afterthefire.co.uk/

[29] *Imagine: Art is child's play*, BBC1, 21st June 2010.

[30] http://www.randomhouse.co.uk/editions/the-train-in-the-night-a-story-of-music-and-loss/9780224093576

[31] http://en.wikipedia.org/wiki/Alice_Herz-Sommer

[32] N. Stokes, *Into the Heart*, Omnibus Press, 1996.

[33] Ibid.

[34] Effective Practice: Play and Exploration, The Early Years Foundation Stage, Crown, 2007

[35] N.T. Wright, *The New Testament and the People of God*, SPCK, 1992.

[36] C.F. Ellis Jr., *Free at Last?: The Gospel in the African-American Experience*, Inter-Varsity Press, 1992.

[37] Ibid.

[38] D. Dark, *Everyday Apocalypse*, Brazos Press, 2002, pps. 12 & 13.

[39] http://jazztheologian.typepad.com/findingthegroove/jazz_theology_101/index.htm

[40] http://jazztheologian.typepad.com/findingthegroove/2009/07/whats-a-jazz-theologian.html

[41] First broadcast Tuesday 09 March 2010

[42] http://www.bbc.co.uk/programmes/b00r6029

[43] Albert Herbert, Robert MacDonald, Modern Painters V2/4.

[44] Albert Herbert, *Introduction* by A.H. in catalogue of his exhibition at England & Co., October 1994.

[45] Ibid.

[46] Ibid.

[47] Ken Kiff, Penelope Bennett, Modern Painters V3/4.

[48] William Anderson, *Cecil Collins: The Quest for the Great Happiness*, Barrie & Jenkins.

[49] *Imagine: Art is child's play*, BBC1, 21.06.2010.

[50] http://commissionformission.blogspot.co.uk/2010/06/tribute-to-peter-shorer.html

[51] Ibid.

[52] G. K. Chesterton, *St Francis of Assisi*, Hodder.

[53] Herald Press, 2003.

[54] Marc Chagall, *My Life*, Peter Owen.

[55] *The Master of the Imaginary*, Camille Bourniquel, *Homage to Chagall*, Leon Amiel Publisher, New York.

[56] F. O'Connor, *Mystery and Manners: Occasional Prose*, Faber & Faber Limited, 1972.

[57] B. Flanaghan, *Written In My Soul*, Omnibus Press, 1990.

[58] M. Guite, *Faith, Hope and Poetry: Theology and the Poetic Imagination*, Ashgate, 2010.

[59] Ibid.

[60] D. Dark, *Everyday Apocalypse*, Brazos Press, 2002.

[61] J. Joyce, *Stephen Hero*, Ed. Theodore Spencer, New Directions Press, 1944.

[62] J. Joyce, *Dubliners*. Ed. Terence Brown. New York: Penguin, 1993.

[63] Ibid.

[64] B. Richards, *Joyce's Epiphany* from *The English Review* http://www.mrbauld.com/epiphany.html.

[65] F. Valente, *Joyce's Dubliner's As Epiphanies*, http://www.themodernword.com/joyce/paper_valente.html

[66] F. O'Connor, *Mystery and Manners: Occasional Prose*, Faber & Faber Limited, 1972.

[67] The last book in the Holy Bible; an apocalyptic vision given to John on the Island of Patmos which ends with an image of the kingdom of God come on earth, as in heaven.

[68] *Artrageous*, Cornerstone Press, 1992.

[69] S. Hipps, *Flickering Pixels: How Technology Shapes Your Faith*, Zondervan, 2009.

[70] Ibid.

[71] Ibid.

[72] T.S. Eliot, *The Waste Land and Other Poems*, R. Malamud ed. Barnes & Noble, 2005.

[73] Ibid.

[74] N. Taylor, *The Velvet Underground in New York, New York in the Velvet Underground*, popMatters.com.

[75] Ibid.

[76] Ibid.

[77] Art of England, September 2009.

[78] Ibid.

[79] David Jones, *The Anathemata*, Faber & Faber Limited.

[80] M. Riddell, *God's home page,* The Bible Reading Fellowship, 1998.

[81] M. Oakley, *The Collage of God*, Darton, Longman and Todd Ltd, 2001.

[82] W. Brueggemann, *The Bible makes sense*, St Mary's Press, 2001,

[83] Ibid.

[84] B. Flanagan, *U2 At the End of the World*, Bantam Press, 1996

[85] J. Waters, *Race of Angels: The Genesis of U2*, Fourth Estate Limited, London, 1994

[86] Ibid.

[87] The Charismatic movement is an ongoing international, cross-denominational Christian movement in which both individual, historically mainstream and entirely new congregations adopt beliefs and practices similar to Pentecostalism.

[88] Christian believers speaking in unknown languages, often thought to be the language of heaven.

[89] D. Lynskey, *Different Class*, Q, Summer 2001.

[90] Van Morrison, *Bringing it all back Home*, New Musical Express 3rd June 1989.

[91] Van Morrison, *See me Through Part II (Just a Closer Walk with Thee)*.

[92] T S Eliot, *The Waste Land*, Faber & Faber.

[93] Derek Hyatt, *Paul Nash and the Megaliths*, Modern Painters, Winter 1994.

[94] Ibid.

[95] David Jones, *The Anathemata*, Faber & Faber Limited.

[96] Nicholas Mosley, *Catastrophe Practice*, Minerva.

[97] Ibid.

[98] Ibid.

[99] Charles Williams, *He came down from Heaven*, Faber & Faber, 1950.

[100] Gunnar Urang, *Shadows of Heaven*.

[101] Ibid.

[102] Charles Williams, *The Greater Trumps*.

[103] See http://www.arcyart.com/ad-truth-to-materials.htm.

[104] http://banksyboy.blogspot.co.uk/2009/08/under-grace.html (click on picture for full effect).

[105] I.F. Walther & R. Metzger, *Chagall*, Taschen, 1987.

[106] Victoria Williams, *Happy Come Home*, Geffen Records, 1993.

[107] I. Stravinsky, *Igor Stravinsky: An Autobiography*, Simon & Schuster, Inc., 1936.

[108] Ibid.

[109] B. Meldhau, *Blank Expressions*, The Guardian Friday 16th September 2011.

[110] Ibid.

[111] Ibid.

[112] A hobo is an itinerant worker. The phrase first began to be used in West USA during the depression.

[113] Beat poetry evolved during the 1940s in both New York City and on the West coast when the end of World War II left poets like Allen Ginsberg, Gary Snyder, Lawrence Ferlinghetti and Gregory Corso questioning mainstream politics and culture.

[114] L. Sloman, Liner Notes to Bob Dylan's *Tell Tale Signs*, Columbia, 2008.

[115] *Sculpting In Time,* University of Texas Press, 1986.

[116] Ibid.

[117] A. Tims, *The artists' artist: modern composers*, The Guardian Wednesday 3rd August 2011.

[118] M. Ainsworth, *Be Still, And Know That I Am God: Concert Halls Rediscover the Sacred*, metanoia.org 2002.

[119] Ibid.

[120] Ibid.

[121] Ibid.

[122] J. Macmillan, *Music and Modernity*, Standpoint November 2009.

[123] B. Bragg, *The Progressive Patriot*, Bantam Press, 2006, p. 199.

[124] Ibid.

[125] Galatians 5 v 25.

[126] M. S. Peck, *The Road Less Travelled: A New Psychology of Love, Traditional Values and Spiritual Growth*, London: Arrow Books Limited, 1990, p. 272.

[127] We are grateful to Hugh Rayment-Pickard for pointing us to Arthur Sullivan's song *The Lost Chord* and Jesus' use of the word *kairos*.

www.thesecretchord.co.uk